SpringerBriefs in Cybersecurity

W0193217

Cybersecurity is a difficult and complex field. The technical, political and legal questions surrounding it are complicated, often stretching a spectrum of diverse technologies, varying legal bodies, different political ideas and responsibilities. Cybersecurity is intrinsically interdisciplinary, and most activities in one field immediately affect the others. Technologies and techniques, strategies and tactics, motives and ideologies, rules and laws, institutions and industries, power and money—all of these topics have a role to play in cybersecurity, and all of these are tightly interwoven.

The SpringerBriefs in Cybersecurity series is comprised of two types of briefs: topic- and country-specific briefs. Topic-specific briefs strive to provide a comprehensive coverage of the whole range of topics surrounding cybersecurity, combining whenever possible legal, ethical, social, political and technical issues. Authors with diverse backgrounds explain their motivation, their mindset, and their approach to the topic, to illuminate its theoretical foundations, the practical nuts and bolts and its past, present and future. Country-specific briefs cover national perceptions and strategies, with officials and national authorities explaining the background, the leading thoughts and interests behind the official statements, to foster a more informed international dialogue.

More information about this series at http://www.springer.com/series/10634

Tatiana Tropina · Cormac Callanan

Self- and Co-regulation in Cybercrime, Cybersecurity and National Security

 Springer

Tatiana Tropina
Max Planck Institute for Foreign and
    International Criminal Law
Freiburg
Germany

Cormac Callanan
Aconite Internet Solutions
Dublin
Ireland

ISSN 2193-973X　　　　　　　　ISSN 2193-9748　(electronic)
SpringerBriefs in Cybersecurity
ISBN 978-3-319-16446-5　　　　　ISBN 978-3-319-16447-2　(eBook)
DOI 10.1007/978-3-319-16447-2

Library of Congress Control Number: 2015935411

Springer Cham Heidelberg New York Dordrecht London
© The Author(s) 2015

Printed on acid-free paper

Springer International Publishing AG Switzerland is part of Springer Science+Business Media
(www.springer.com)

Foreword

The Internet is everywhere. It stretches across all layers of society, involving the civil society, the business community and governments. And it is not just consumed, but also operationally used, created, maintained and changed by all these different actors. It is enabling them if they master it, and disabling or disadvantaging them if it does not work properly.

Now all of these actors desire basic values such as security, freedom and privacy, and of course they would like them implemented in the Internet, too. Different cultures may have different perceptions about priorities and interpretations of these values, but they still want them implemented in some way. Yet implementing these values requires changes in this environment. Technologies, business modalities, innovation or widely accepted use-models will have to be revised and remodelled to some extent, and many of these revisions will involve trade-offs with other actors' interests.

Accordingly, the question of who should be the bringer and carrier of this change is the cornerstone of a heated debate. A lot of actors are reluctant to engage in change at all, as they benefit from the current, unregulated model and mainly oppose any emergence of other actors. These other actors—mostly disadvantaged entities or institutions in formal responsibility for according issues—at their end are trying to identify and enforce levers to change the established landscape. The result is a regulatory and lobbying battle raging behind the colourful outer shell of the web.

The authors of this brief, Tropina and Callanan, embarked on the mission to map out this contested landscape, its actors, their stakes and interests. This is a challenging undertaking, as many of these entities and their dynamics are not very visible, especially in their entanglements and undercurrents, but Tropina and Callanan managed to identify and analyse them with high granularity. Moreover, the authors provide a profound theoretical analysis of the effectiveness and efficiency of different regulatory approaches, focusing in particular on industrial attempts of self-regulation or the more forthcoming variant of public–private co-regulation, deriving general conclusions and creating recommendations with high value for anybody working in or on this field.

At the present time of an ever more contested Internet, this contribution could hardly be more relevant, and I assume it will have an impact on the ongoing process and the debates surrounding it.

February 2015   Dr. Sandro Gaycken
                                                                              ESMT Berlin

Contents

**2   Evolution, Implementation and Practice of Internet
Self-regulation, Co-regulation and Public–Private
Collaboration** 43

Cormac Callanan

Chapter 1
Public–Private Collaboration: Cybercrime, Cybersecurity and National Security

Tatiana Tropina

Abstract This chapter analyses theoretical and practical implications of different forms of self- and co-regulation in the field of cybersecurity. In the past decade, the approaches to cybersecurity and critical information infrastructure protection have been based on the notion of the necessity for public–private collaboration, multi-faceted strategies and recognition of the significant role that industry plays in securing the information networks. However, with the raise of cybersecurity on the top of the policy agenda, many governments and academics are concerned with the possible failure of the private sector in delivering acceptable level of security in the information networks without governmental intervention. This shift of the concept has lead to the proposals to legislate cybersecurity in the form of mandatory reporting of security incidents and obligations to share information, security stan-dards and compliance procedures. One of such proposals is currently being dis-cussed as EU NIS directive. These developments raise many concerns about shifting the balance in cybersecurity from bottom-up voluntary approaches and collaboration to a heavier regulation. This chapter argues that this turn can have negative consequences and that the best way to provide cybersecurity is the evolvement of the existing channels for collaboration and building trust between industry and governments.

Keywords Cybercrime · Cybersecurity

1.1 Introduction

The ecosystem of fighting cybercrime and maintaining cybersecurity nowadays consists of interdependent international and national actors linked to national information infrastructure networks and services, including financial and banking systems, energy supply and communication networks. The overall development and innovation of the ICT networks has been, and is largely, dominated and controlled by private industry with little or no regulation or statutory intervention involved. As a result, private rather than public actors often fund, manage and run Internet and

© The Author(s) 2015   1
T. Tropina and C. Callanan, *Self- and Co-regulation in Cybercrime,*
Cybersecurity and National Security, SpringerBriefs in Cybersecurity,
DOI 10.1007/978-3-319-16447-2_1

communication networks, including critical information infrastructure. This situation calls for new cooperative models of regulation and enforcement between governments and private industry on different levels—national, regional and international. It raises the challenge of developing effective approaches to co- and self-regulation to address offences in cyberspace and make information infrastructure resilient and safe.

With the technical, legal, business complexity of the environment, cybersecurity regulation looks like an intricate riddle. International organisations, national governments, academics, businesses and technical communities are trying to bring the pieces of this puzzle together and reach an agreement on how and who should regulate and protect the cyberworld. Though there is a common understanding that governments cannot supply an adequate level of cybersecurity and fight cybercrime on their own without an involvement of the private sector, there are still fierce discussions on how the industry shall be involved, what is the role of the direct government intervention in this regard, whether the industry should be encouraged or coerced to cooperate and if multi-stakeholder bottom-up approaches can guarantee an adequate level of security of the information networks. The policy dilemma continues brewing without clarity: with all the efforts taken to find a solution to a cybersecurity regulation in the recent years, there is neither a general agreement nor clear answers. The current state of cybersecurity regulation looks like a patchwork of solutions found out rather as a response to the urgent problems than any structured approaches.

Since the 1990s, with the involvement of the Internet service providers (ISPs) to the voluntary cooperation on fighting illegal content online, many forms of public–private collaboration, such as hotlines, industry codes of conducts, awareness raising programs, cooperation agreements between industry and the governments and—later—some successful attempts to establish wide-national cross-sector cooperation in some countries gave a promise of the possible supply of cybersecurity in a form of public–private partnerships. In this regard, the common notion, which dominated in the past several years on the policy making and business level, is that cybersecurity and critical information infrastructure protection require public–private collaboration, multifaceted strategies, hands-off regulation and recognition of the significant role that industry plays in securing the information networks. However, the raising dependency on critical information infrastructures and concerns about the consequences of possible disruptions to the point of catastrophic scenarios made a turn in the policy making and made for the calls for hierarchical top-down command-and-control solutions. The recent discussions and legislative developments, especially on the level of the EU and its member states, raise many concerns among industry and academics about shifting the balance in cybersecurity from bottom-up voluntary approaches and collaboration to a heavier regulation. The rationale behind the attempts of some governments and supranational organisations like the EU to find a regulatory solution to protect critical information infrastructure and the safety of the citizens online is quite reasonable. Cyber-threats have become a reality, and they can possibly have drastic consequences. However, there is still a debate if the move away from voluntary collaboration to a statutory intervention could have even more negative effect to the supply of cybersecurity than no regulation at all.

The current policy and academic discussions in context of the new regulatory developments are mostly debating the issue of the efficiency of public–private partnerships. What gets missing and overlooked in this debate is that there are other forms of co- and self-regulation that have proven to be successful models of industry involvement in cybersecurity. Existing channels of cooperation, information sharing and enforcement might still be in their infancy, suffer from imperfections and be in a need for improvements. However, any debate on whether self- and co-regulation is efficient should, first of all, take into account the existence of different forms of collaboration in addition to public–private partnerships, and, secondly, recognise that cybersecurity includes different domains and areas, which require complex solutions. There is no single "one-size-fits-all" approach.

This chapter analyses the current and potential approaches to self- and co-regulation in fighting cybercrime and providing cybersecurity. It analyses different forms of cooperation—from ad hoc and accidental collaboration to the structured approaches. Furthermore, it examines the issue of the balance between hands-off regulation and statutory intervention and analyses the problems and drawbacks of different forms of regulation.

Section 1.2 of this chapter discusses misconceptions related to the terms "cybercrime", "national security", "cyberwar" and consequences of the lack of clear distinction between them. It frames further discussion on the self- and co-regulatory measures in the field of cybersecurity by referring to various domains of regulation and highlighting the problems, which arise from the blurring borders between law enforcement and civil and military defence.

Section 1.3, firstly, provides insights into the historical development of co-regulation and self-regulation as forms of public–private collaboration against cybercrime in the multi-stakeholder environment. It refers to the evolving nature of cyber-threats and explains the complexity of the cybersecurity ecosystem. Secondly, it analyses the differences between theoretical approaches to self- and co-regulation and practical implications of public–private collaboration. Thirdly, it analyses the emerging trend of legislating cybersecurity.

Section 1.4 examines existing types of collaboration between governments and industries at the national and international levels, such as national public–private cybercrime platforms, public–private partnerships on tackling particular problems, industry codes of conduct and emerging models of wide-national and international public–private cooperation initiatives in cybersecurity.

Section 1.5 discusses the problems that existing forms of public–private collaboration may encounter. One of the main issues covered in this section is the degree of governmental intervention and the disadvantages of the recent turn from collaborative bottom-up approach to the statutory intervention. It expresses concerns that the shift from encouraging voluntary collaboration to coercion is a dangerous setback in fighting cybercrime and maintaining cybersecurity. Furthermore, the section analyses such problems of public–private cooperation as limitations related to the mandate of the governments, human rights and safeguards, transparency, accountability, costs and incentives. Finally, the section concludes with answering the question where governmental intervention is an option for making cyberworld safe and secure.

1.2 Cybersecurity, Cybercrime, Cyberwar? Terminology and Misconceptions

Public–private collaboration in the field of cybersecurity includes many private stakeholders involved in a broad range of activities—from hotlines for takedown of illegal content to wide-nation programmes on critical information infrastructure protection, from ad hoc collaboration on tracing child abuse online rings to the jointly funded projects on botnet mitigation. However, despite the success of many of the public–private cooperation projects, there are currently debates about inefficiency of the public–private collaboration and the need of tougher regulatory schemes in cybersecurity. Sceptical voices are mostly raised because of national security concerns. While in the field of fighting cybercrime there is a general agreement that public–private collaboration is the only way to tackle various form of online criminal activity, the discussions on public–private partnerships in cybersecurity are bringing and supporting the opposite point of view: according to some studies, industry is rather reluctant to participate in joint activities, the goals of the public and private sectors are not matching, and public–private partnerships have more limitations that benefits. This discussion will be further addressed in the chapter on the forms of government intervention. However, before starting any debate, it is necessary to understand which domain the "cybersecurity" cooperation actually belongs to. The mixed opinions about benefits of public–private partnerships in cybersecurity come from the misunderstanding of the fact that such partnerships are operating in distinct areas that represent different, though overlapping due to the nature of cyberspace, domains of various governmental bodies.

As is it pointed out by Nye [1], despite the attempts to picture a cyberspace as an "ungoverned lawless Wild West" [1: p. 14], the cyber domain involves various forms of regulation—from strict forms such as government-lead control by the means of criminal law and criminal procedure law related to cybercrime to multi-dimensional multi-stakeholder forms of governance such as ICANN and Internet Engineering Task Force. Cybersecurity is one of the domains where frameworks for governance do exist, though being managed by different public and private stakeholders. The problems of collaboration in providing cybersecurity arise because the security of information networks is a very complex and multifaceted matter, which has, depending on the field governed, different dimensions and various implications for the governance.

One of the biggest issues in any cybersecurity governance debate is the use of the generic term "cybersecurity". This "umbrella" term can conflate security problems that might be similar in their technical nature but will have very different consequences in terms of law and regulation and, thus, different set of solutions [2].

The cybersecurity-related terms, such as "cybercrime", "cyberwar", "cyberattack" and "cyberterrorism", in the absence of a clear consensus with regard to their meaning and relative novelty of these terms, are used interchangeably [3] and "with little regard for what they are meant to include" [4]. This practice creates confusion and misunderstanding as to what the issue actually is and which form of legal and regulatory response shall address it. "Sensationalisation" [3] and exaggeration [5: 2] of certain cybercrimes which come from the overuse of terms such as "cyberwar" and "cyber-weapons", the tendency to "view the situation in catastrophic terms" [6], further contribute to the confusion in distinguishing law enforcement and national security domains.

This perplexity has negative consequences for public–private collaboration, because the forms of cooperation, which are successful in one of the areas of law and regulation, can fail or can hardly be leveraged to another domain. The areas of regulation, such as law enforcement, civil defence and military defence, do overlap because of the nature of cyberspace; however, confusing them can cause misinterpretation with regard to the goals of collaboration, set of stakeholders involved and incentives for both public and private parties. Thus, in the debate on the successfulness of cooperation between governments and private sector in the field of cybersecurity, it is very important to understand in which field cooperation is being carried out.

The misinterpretation of different terms and domains, such as fighting cybercrime, protecting critical information infrastructure and national security, worsens due to the absence of a fine line between these fields. The same technical tools can be used in cyberspace to commit profit-driven crimes and carry out the acts that can be legitimately treated as national security concerns by many governments. For example, the botnets are widely used for committing profit-driven crimes and are one of the tools the cybercrime industry uses to flourish; however, they have also been used for politically motivated attacks and cyber-espionage [7]. The problem of blurring boundaries further contributes to the uncertainty as to how and who shall govern cybersecurity, what are the applicable legal and regulatory regimes and which roles private stakeholders will be playing in safeguarding cyberspace.

Analysis provided in this chapter does not serve the purpose to define cybercrime, cybersecurity and cyberwar—this task would require much more space since, first of all, there is no agreed definition of all those terms [8, 9], and, secondly, there are still debates on the applicability of the term cyberwar in the framework of international law [8]. Further discussion serves the purpose to show the blurring borders between different cybersecurity-related domains and confusions associated with this uncertainty.

1.2.1 Cybersecurity: Different Dimensions and Blurring Borders

The set of threats emerging in cyberspace blurs the boundaries between several areas, which traditionally were considered to be distinct fields of policy and regulation. First of all, the division between internal and external order [10], and as a result of the dichotomy of internal and external policies [11], is being undermined due to the transnational nature of cyberspace. Traditionally, maintaining the public order required law enforcement and criminal justice for internal order and military force and international agreements for mitigation of external threats [10]. Cyberthreats, which can originate from abroad or from the same city and target both external and internal order, are sometimes very hard to be clearly attributed to one of the policy domains.

Secondly, this complexity further increases with the blurring borders between the fields that traditionally used to have a clear distinction: civil defence, military defence and criminal justice (law enforcement) [11, 12]. The fading of boundaries in this field has been caused by the change that cyberspace brings to the concept of aggression and crime. The traditional notion mostly referred to aggression and acts committed in the physical world for both crimes and war. In the case of breach of criminal law, there was a clear domain for criminal justice and policing to prevent crime and to prosecute the offender with the ultimate dominance of reactive approach [8]. This sphere of responsibility was clearly defined by the statutory regulation. It mostly required application of the national law of the sovereign state, and, if there was international component, collaboration between law enforcement agencies across the borders. Mutual legal assistance treaties were mostly enough as a mechanism for assistance in the case of cross-border crime.

The same concept of physical aggression played an important role in the field of war conflict between the states. Brenner [10: 403] highlights that "war is unambiguous in the real-world because it is unique; only nation-states can summon the resources needed to launch a physical land, sea, or air attack on another nation-state". Aggression for the purpose of military defence meant a physical attack or a threat of it, referred to the territorial issues. This concept allowed for defining the regulatory and policy domain responsible for defence and the applicable legal regime in the case of war.

However, nowadays, because of the anonymity of the Internet and the blurring borders between state and non-state actors, it is much more difficult to make a clear distinction both for the purpose of prevention of and reaction to the cybersecurity threats. States can initiate cybercrimes and cyber-espionage, politically motivated individuals can launch cyberattacks that cannot be attributed to any foreign governments and organised crime groups can tackle businesses to the degree that make it a threat to economic well-being of the nation. The questions that rise in this regard still remain unanswered. How to attribute the cyber-espionage to a particular state? How to distinguish prevention of hacker attacks, which are not backed by state parties (hacktivism) or from state-organised cyber-aggression? Does cross-border surveillance or breaking into the networks carried out by a foreign government constitute a crime or an act of aggression or is there no legal regime applicable to this kind of behaviour?

Theoretically, the domains can be distinguished based on the nature of threats and approaches to addressing them. One of the ways to draw a line is the "two-stream" model suggested by Maurer [13]. His research differentiates two international (on the level of the UN) approaches to the cybersecurity issues: the politico-military stream and the economic stream. The former refers to the use of information technologies for undermining international stability, and the latter includes the criminal misuse of information technologies [13]. This distinction is further supported by Jang and Lim [14], who discuss two main common approaches to the cyber-threats: security-oriented approach that considers cyberattacks as a threat to national security and law enforcement approach that brings the issue of attacks to the domain of criminal justice. The former relates to the efforts to deter and prevent, and the latter focuses on investigation, attribution and prosecution.

While this distinction certainly exists and, moreover, allows drawing a line for the purpose of this analysis, some of the types of "crimes" are debatable concerning how they fall into either economic crime or national security category. For example, while economic espionage can be attributed to cybercrime [14] when it is profit-driven, there are growing concerns that this type of spying on companies can threaten national security, especially when committed by state-sponsored actors [15]. In May 2014, US Department of Justice charged five Chinese citizens with hacking into the networks of the US companies. The indictment linked the espionage to the Chinese government and named members of Unit 61,398 and identified them as the members of the Shanghai-based cyberunit of the People's Liberation Army.[1] This has been the first attempt so far to attribute economic espionage to people "behind the screen" and, moreover, to link the acts not only to particular people, but also to the foreign government. It is outside of the scope of this chapter to make political or legal judgements of this case. However, it does show how the borders between the "national security" stream and the "crime" stream are blurring.

Another example of the efforts to bring national security case to the domain of criminal justice is the investigation into electronic mass surveillance of EU citizens carried out by the Committee on Civil Liberties, Justice and Home Affairs of the EU Parliament. At one of the hearings on the allegations of NSA tapping into the SWIFT database, issues were raised with regard to the involvement of Europol in investigation of the NSA activities and the mandate of Europol in cybercrime investigations. Answering the questions, the Director of Europol, Rob Wainwright, stated that, firstly, no EU member state had made a request to investigate NSA activities, and, secondly, Europol has no mandate to investigate any state espionage allegations. As a result of the inquiry, the European Parliament adopted a resolution of 12 March 2014 "On the US NSA surveillance programme, surveillance bodies in various Member States and their impact on EU citizens' fundamental rights and on transatlantic cooperation in Justice and Home Affairs [2013/2188(INI)]" calling for the "full use" of the mandate of Europol for requesting the competent authorities of the member states to investigate cyberattacks with cross-border impact and, if necessary, enhancing this mandate to allow initiation of Europol's own

---

[1]The full text of the indictment can be accessed on the website on the US Department of Justice: http://www.justice.gov/iso/opa/resources/5122014519132358461949.pdf.

investigations.[2] In addition to illustrating the tension between mandates of criminal law and national security, this case constitutes yet another attempt to bring two domains together and investigate the national security threats under the mandate of criminal justice.

Some of the experts even say that the distinction is not relevant anymore because the focus should be put on the methodology of the attacks, targets and consequences [12]. This assertion can, to some extent, be true concerning the tools and consequences of the attacks, especially for the private sector in relation to damage control and risk mitigation [3]. However, there is still a relevance of drawing if not clear, but a cleaner line between law enforcement and national security to clarify the "ownership of cybersecurity" [4] to understand which entities should deal with the incident: national security agencies, military or law enforcement [8].

One of the possible options to make a relevant distinction is a criminal attribution. However, attribution also represents a certain challenge due to anonymity of the Internet. Evidently, it is only attribution that can provide the information on whether the source of attack is a criminal or a state actor and define the domain of criminal justice and national security according to the nature of the threat [3]. Yet there is one factor that is difficult to find out, namely motivation of the criminal. Motivation plays an important role: a person behind the cyberattack might be stand-alone criminal backed up by the government or politically motivated hacktivist, or someone with terrorist motives.

Does attribution help to separate domains for the purpose of providing cyber-security? On one hand, it might be (theoretically) useful to use the attribution for distinguishing different types of security threats, such as national security and crime—this will at least allow defining the domain of cooperation such as criminal justice/national security. On the other hand, attribution itself is in many cases difficult, if not impossible because of the anonymity of the Internet and its trans-border nature. Furthermore, attribution requires some efforts of investigating the attack. It means that in order to be attributed and to fall within one of the domains, be it national security or law enforcement, the attack should be investigated first, but it is unclear whether law enforcement or national security entities have to carry out the investigation. Thus, the question of attribution, though being very important for practical purposes—from investigation and prosecution of cybercrime to iden-tifying the risk trends and developing adequate responses in the national security area—can be only of theoretical importance when it comes to drawing a clear distinction between different domains.

It is evident that, despite all the attempts to draw distinction between security mandates using the concepts of criminal law, law of armed conflict and public international law, the whole concept of cybersecurity does not fit traditional concepts used for this distinction [6]. There is a complex set of factors, which assigns a particular problem to the law enforcement or to the agencies responsible for the

---

[2]The full text of the resolution is available at: http://www.europarl.europa.eu/sides/getDoc.do?type=TA&language=EN&reference=P7-TA-2014-0230.

national security: seriousness of the threat, possible consequences and the scale of the particular problem, just to name a few. Moreover, both national security and crime control bodies may consider the same cybersecurity issue from different angles as a part of their domain. Again, one of the good examples is the risks associated with the use of botnets: they are considered to be a concern for law-enforcement agencies because of being used for commission of profit-driven crimes and for national security agencies due to the role they can play in politically motivated attacks and economic espionage [7].

1.2.2 Areas of Public–Private Collaboration on Cybersecurity

The uncertainty, which arises from the blurring borders between cybercrime and national security, has negative effects on the progress of the public–private collaboration in the field of cybersecurity on both policy and operation levels. With blurring borders, ambiguous domains, absence of clear definitions of what crime and cyberwar are and attribution issues, it is hard to develop successful frameworks for collaboration. To understand clearly which private entities and in what way should be involved in addressing particular problem, it is necessary to have an idea which government entities are responsible for a particular issue.

There have been attempts to distinguish domains by, for example, identifying priority areas, like it has been done by the EU Cybersecurity Strategy, which sets several priorities: achieving cyber-resilience, reducing cybercrime, developing cyber defence policy and capabilities; developing industrial and technological resources for cybersecurity and establishing a coherent international cyberspace policy. This division is pretty much in line with the distinction made in academic literature for example, Klimburg [16] distinguishes several mandates in national cybersecurity: military cyber, countering cybercrime, intelligence and counter-intelligence, critical information infrastructure protection, cyber diplomacy and Internet governance, with each of them being addressed by different departments within the nation state. Klimburg [16] argues that despite the fact that the areas of cybersecurity represent different facets of the same problem, each of the fields has its distinct focus and lexicon.

Further difficulties arise from lack of the agreement on what constitutes cybersecurity and what this term actually encompasses. There is no internationally accepted definition of cybersecurity (for example, EU Cybersecurity Strategy does not define it), so the understanding of this term differs from one nation state to another. Cybersecurity can be referred to as a broad concept, which includes security both in online and offline world, or narrowed down only to online safety [17]. Confusion might grow when the meaning of cybersecurity is limited to safeguards and actions to protect networks and information infrastructure with regard to their integrity, availability and confidentiality (CIA crimes). For example, some studies [18] in this regard contend that cybersecurity should be focused on technology-based and code-based threats and should be limited to the crimes that are committed against computers (CIA crimes) and with exclusion of the crimes, which are merely facilitated by the use of computers. If we apply this theory to the public–private collaboration in cybersecurity, the concept of CIA threats covers a wide range of activities related both to civilian and military fields. However, it excludes some very important forms of cooperation related to the illegal content crimes such as online child abuse images and terrorist content. Illegal content does not represent a technical cybersecurity threat since it does not interfere with networks and systems. However, hardly anyone would debate the importance of the fight against child abuse. When cooperation in the field of cybersecurity is limited to technical threats only, a wide range of activities can be excluded and overlooked despite the fact that the initial involvement of the private industry in fighting cybercrime started with creation of hotlines for removal of child abuse content.

Collaboration in the field of cybercrime does not always include technical aspects of cybersecurity and protection of networks and systems. For example, fighting online child abuse, despite the requirement of technical knowledge and use of the technical tools for investigating crimes and detecting offenders, has different object of legal protection than technical security of the networks and vice versa, not every cybersecurity effort would be related to cybercrime. Investigation and prosecution of crimes as a domain of law enforcement will represent just a narrow field in this complex issue of cybersecurity in addition to bringing criminal acts of committing the cyberattacks to criminal justice domain, the efforts of different stakeholders in cybersecurity ecosystem will include deterrence, network resilience, collection of information on the type of attacks, attribution to the source without prosecution, just to name a few.

This book chapter approaches the issue of public–private collaboration from a broad perspective and focuses on different forms and areas of cooperation, including tackling the problem of cybercrime, protection of critical information infrastructure and national security. For the purpose of this analysis, the first area—cybercrime—covers not only crimes committed against confidentiality, integrity and availability of computer systems, but also content crimes (such as child abuse images and terrorist content) and any other types of crimes committed online. Public–private cooperation in this field can be attributed to "criminal justice domain" and includes prosecution, investigation, detection and an early disruption of crimes committed online, be it crimes against confidentiality, integrity and availability of data or computer-facilitated crimes or crimes related to illegal content. Collaboration in this area is based on the criminal law and criminal procedural law, legal frameworks on the liability of the intermediaries and partially on preventive police law.

The second area of cooperation is the involvement of the private sector in national security. As a distinct field from the criminal justice, it refers to collaboration between industry and governments on such security concerns as politically motivated attacks, economic espionage and serious threats. The third field is alliances between private stakeholders and regulators on cyber-resilience and critical information infrastructure protection. The distinct feature of this area, though it can be considered as part of national security concerns, is that the threats for critical information do not necessarily involve malicious intent. Critical information infrastructure protection includes resilience to weather disasters, technical failures and human errors.

It is hard to separate these three fields clearly, because they are overlapping. However, with this separation (even if the borders are blurring), a certain field of regulation can at least be distinguished and attributed to the particular agencies depending on the country: cybercrime to law enforcement, national security to the governmental bodies such as foreign ministries and intelligence services and critical information infrastructure protection to certain type regulators.

Another important factor is that the same private stakeholders can play multiple roles: one global service provider or financial institution can be a part of public–private partnership programmes in all three areas. For example, such global service providers such as Microsoft and Google are the owners of their internal technological infrastructure, providers of services to their customers, personal data controllers and processors; they can participate in ad hoc cooperation with law enforcement agencies on investigating a particular case, or collaborate on capacity-building programmes, or get involved in the analysis of the threats related to national security.

The participation of private industry in all three fields is necessary but has different dimensions and consequences. While there is a widely accepted notion that government cannot and shall not be expected to fight cybercrime and provide cybersecurity alone, there is a common misunderstanding about the role of the industry in the aforementioned fields, and, as a consequence, unmet expectations and the failure of leveraging good practices and core competences from one area to another. The fundamental problem is that distinct laws regulate those fields and the role of the industry would be different for each of these areas. While many public–private collaboration initiatives reached some degree of success in the criminal justice domain, they cannot yet enjoy the same level of success in the national security field, which tends to be less inclusive. Misconceptions arise when the areas of regulation are mixed, because national security tends to have higher political priority, less number of stakeholders involved in decision-making process and less transparency. According to the study carried out by OECD [19], businesses and civil society are concerned with the trend of increasingly blurring borders between national security and economic/social security and warfare semantics, because this absence of separation can bring "challenging consequences", such as additional burdens, lack of transparency and less openness.

1.3 Regulating Cybersecurity: What Are the Options?

Before the evolvement of information and communication technologies, fighting crime and providing public security was mostly considered as a domain of national governments. Both criminal law and national security imply sovereignty issues, the duty of the state to protect its citizens and mechanisms of enforcement of the legal and policy frameworks, which require hierarchical structures and command-and-control approaches.

The problem of fighting cybercrime and protecting national interests in cyberspace, in the first place, reflects the tension between non-flexible legal frameworks—which, like criminal law, were not meant to be flexible by their nature—and the non-hierarchical structure and the borderless nature of the information and communication networks that do not fit the traditional top-down command-and-control models. The decentralised architecture of the Internet is eroding old paradigms of the division of responsibilities between government, private sector and civil society, also because in general, the concept of Internet governance has been largely dominated by the idea of a multi-stakeholder model. This transformation of the role of regulators and nation states in governing one of the biggest "enabler" of the modern economy and the idea of hands-off regulation for the sake of technological development allowed the Internet to flourish and penetrate all areas of business and social life.

1.3.1 Cybersecurity as a Multi-stakeholder Environment: Transformation

Until the beginning of 2000s, governments and law enforcement agencies mostly had to intervene only when information security failed and crime happened—the main agenda for the public sector was to criminalise the new types of threats, such as crimes against confidentiality, integrity and availability of computer data and systems, to equip law enforcement agencies with tools—both technical and legal—to investigate and prosecute the new types of infringements and to harmonise substantive criminal law and procedural frameworks on the international level to avoid creations of safe havens for cybercriminals. On this stage, industry was considered mostly as collaborator for investigations or for taking down illegal content online, and it was mainly the ISPs who got involved as a focal point for cooperation. With the growing number of Internet users and, as a result, increasing cybercrime rates, it was obvious that centralised state intervention can often fail to address the problem, because criminals can easily bypass traditional regulatory frameworks in transborder cyberspace [20: 1]. Due to the low reporting rates of cybercrime and cyberattacks [21: 69], it became extremely difficult for governments and law enforcement agencies to detect cybercrime on their own: due to the lack of resources, they could do little more than investigate and prosecute only a "tiny fraction" [22: 5] of cybercrime, let alone follow the complex and constantly changing landscape of cyber-threats. As a consequence, states are increasingly engaging in partnerships with the private sector to tackle cybercrime [23, 24], and co-regulatory and self-regulatory measures were sometimes appraised as being even more effective than criminal law and its enforcement [25]. This trend started in the 1990s with the creation of the first private hotlines for reporting illegal content, mainly related to child abuse, as it will be discussed in Chap. 2 of this edition.

Nowadays, self- and co-regulatory approaches exist in many areas of fighting cybercrime both on national and international levels.

However, till the end of the 1990s, when the threat of the millennium software bug attracted a lot of attention, the concept of "cybersecurity" as well as the term itself was not common [16: 12]. National governments were busy struggling with applying old legal frameworks to fighting cybercrime, striving to find new models to involve the private stakeholders in cooperation and trying to define the borders of responsibilities of the intermediaries for illegal content, were mostly leaving the issue of cybersecurity with regard to securing networks and infrastructure to the private sector. One of the important aspects, which set the paradigm for this approach, was the fact that with the commercialisation of the NSFNet in the 1990s, the US government moved the development and management of the infrastructure to the business and non-profit organisations and applied hands-off model to the internet governance, leaving the governance of the domain name system to the private entity—ICANN [26, 27].

The whole development of the Internet was dominated by commercial interests and market forces and followed by the principle of imposing no regulation for the sake of faster development. In this context, the private sector was considered to have enough knowledge and experience to provide security of its networks. Moreover, the private entities were in general opposing any attempts to regulate the Internet because of the general perception that regulation is too slow and government intervention can hamper the development of new technologies [27]. This approach has proven to be a great success for the evolution of the information and communication technologies: in just a few years, industry has developed fast and cost-effective solutions for providing connection and services. Internet boosted economic growth, penetrated all the areas of social life and economy, and, ultimately, became an essential part of everyday life and—as a turning point—brought the growing dependency on information infrastructures. This interdependency of different critical infrastructures, both public and private (banking, energy supply, information technologies, etc.), and their increasing dependence on information networks, which made them vulnerable to crimes and attacks [28, 29], dramatically changed the cybersecurity landscape. New types of attacks such as botnets, where automation plays an important role, brought complex challenges for prevention, detection and investigation of the new types of crimes and new concerns about the possible drastic effects that even a short disruption of the functioning of critical information infrastructures can have. This can be considered as a turning point with regard to reconsidering the role of the governments in cybersecurity field and recognising the cybersecurity issues as one of the high priorities on political agenda.

The consequences of these developments are twofold. On one hand, this increasing complexity drove the development of the new cooperative models for addressing the new challenges and shifted focus from cybercrime and reactive approach (investigation and prosecution) to a far-reaching concept of cybersecurity, which includes also proactive measures such as prevention, detection, awareness raising and information sharing. On the other hand, the pictures of catastrophic scenarios "have produced a rush to regulate cybersecurity" [6]. A possibility of a failure and drastic consequences made policy makers question the reliability of hands-off regulation and consider stronger involvement of the governments into the provision of cybersecurity [26].

This transformation has changed the scene of addressing the problem of cybersecurity into a "complex policy issue, which requires solutions at various levels, both national and international, and by means both non-governmental and governmental" [18]. The ecosystem of cybersecurity itself poses a big challenge: the fast and mostly unregulated development of the information and communication technologies resulted in the "existence of myriad actors in the information security field" [30: 143]. The complexity of this ecosystem raises new issues of determining roles and domains of different stakeholders involved in tackling cybercrime and securing a safe cyber-environment. The growing number of Internet economy intermediaries—not only ISPs but also e-commerce and m-commerce companies, e-payment providers, application developers and software vendors, critical information infrastructure operators and others—became "critical nodes" for preventing and investigating cybercrime and safeguarding security of their systems and networks in their respective sectors [31: 196]. Whether governments want it or not, the fact that cyber infrastructure was built and is owned by private sector and the whole structure of decentralised networks and their history of non-hierarchical regulation make the cybersecurity ecosystem a flexible multi-stakeholder environment with no single entity on the top which can control and manage the processes. The idea that no single government can provide cybersecurity using only its own capabilities without involving private sector has thus become "conventional wisdom" [32: 85].

However, despite the general agreement that governments on their own can make only "poor enablers" of cybersecurity [33] and call for cooperation and multi-stakeholder approaches, there is no clear idea with regard to the models of cooperation. Technical complexity of the digital ecosystem, heterogeneity of stakeholders involved in different layers across jurisdictions, blurring borders between external and internal policy and public and private matters and absence of clear distinction between law enforcement, civil defence and military defence create the situation of regulatory uncertainty which delays the development of effective regulatory solutions [11, 34, 35]. Due to the convergence of services and uncertainty of legal regimes applicable to different cyber-threats (crime, national security, intelligence), regulatory spheres can superimpose and mandates of different agencies dealing with cybercrime and cybersecurity can overlap. Until now, there is no widely accepted model of the distribution of regulatory responsibilities in the ecosystem of cybersecurity answering the question who shall regulate and what [36]. For example, despite the current attempts of the European Union to create homogeneous approach to cyberecurity, the system of mandates of different stakeholders and regulatory bodies in this field in the EU looks like an extremely complex puzzle, where "no-one…has a clear understanding of how all the different pieces fit together" [37: 17]. The international dimension of a problem and the fact that national states can have conflicting security interests further contribute to the increasing complexity of the regulatory challenge [38, 39: 430].

Bearing in mind this uncertainty of regulatory domains, some studies suggest that the new models of regulation should be developed to address cybersecurity problems. The World Bank Group [40: 3–4, 41] suggests that the ecosystem of cybersecurity is moving to the network model: it suggests that instead of focusing on institutions and functions (who shall do and what), the focus has to be shifted to the processes (e.g. fighting SPAM or creation of computer emergency response centres), procedures and information flows between different institutions. Network model refers, instead of specific agencies, to bodies (nodes) performing different functions in the ecosystem of cyberseurity and sharing—formally or informally—information and practices. The network model of the cybercrime and cybersecurity ecosystem, where hierarchical structures of governance are not applicable any more or have to be complemented, raises the challenge of creating better regulatory approaches in which the central question is, how cooperative governance can achieve the desired outcomes of reduction, detection and investigation of crimes. Dupont [34] refers to the "nodal" regulation and the concept of regulatory pluralism which is based on the belief that "by relying on diverse, complementary and self-reinforcing regulatory instruments, policies can be implemented in a manner that is more responsive to the specific context, resources and constraints of a particular sector" as to one of the possible ways to address cybersecurity problems. Gercke et al. [36] and Tropina [42] suggest the concept of "smart regulation", which will be able to analyse the threats, to detect if intervention is needed and to develop new tools for dealing with the problems instead of applying old means that were not meant to regulate a decentralised environment. All these models assume that the gap between traditional models of governmental intervention and complex technological environment can be bridged only by approaching it with the new flexible cooperative models that include both public and private stakeholders and can combine the nodes of both legal and extra-legal regulation and facilitate the "reflexive and cohesive approach" [43: 19] to cybersecurity—necessary in a transnational decentralised network world.

While national governments have the power to establish and enforce legal and regulatory frameworks, the private sector understands the changing and converging nature of the ICT environment and has greater adaptability towards new technologies and services. Private actors have more expertise and resources and possess the necessary knowledge to investigate cybercrime and single out relevant cybersecurity threats, analyse them and produce an adequate response to them [11]. The private sector's knowledge and adaptability complement the resources and expertise of the government in the enforcement of criminal law, crime investigation and governments' mandate in foreign policy and diplomacy.

However, despite the clear need for mutual support between the governments and the private sector in cybersecurity and cybercrime field, the "ways and means of this assistance are fiercely debated" [16]. The concept on how to achieve the involvement of the private industry varies significantly in terms of approaches to the degree of governmental intervention, combination of regulatory tools and economic and policy incentives. In general, three ways can be identified, but they are often confused concerning their nature: regulation, co-regulation and self-regulation. Interestingly, despite the general acknowledgement of the need for state and private sector to partner with each other, in many cases, suggested approaches to such "partnerships" rather tend to be governmental intervention rather than cooperation, when duties and responsibilities are imposed on private actors with some degree of control from the governments. One of the prominent examples in this regard is the EU Cybersecurity Strategy, which is calling for a collaborative approach between industry and governments to secure the cyberspace. However, despite this declaration, one of the measures the strategy proposes is obligatory reporting of security breaches, which, of course, implies the participation of the private sector in the information sharing, but excludes the voluntary element and uses the coercion instead. Such measures cannot be attributed to collaboration or partnerships since they are just an example of a pure statutory regulation. This is why it is necessary to understand what self- and co-regulation is and what it is not.

1.3.2 Self- and Co-regulation: Theoretical Approaches and Practical Implementation

The shift from the concept of information security driven mostly by market demand to the cybersecurity as a part of policy agenda happened in the beginning of the 2000s [44]. This turn was caused by the growing critique of hands-off concept caused by the governments' concerns about protecting critical information infrastructures. The change of attitude raised a question as to what kind of model of regulation is applicable to the increasingly unruly cyberworld. The choice between top-down hierarchical approach and completely bottom-up approach or a combination of these two can be generally considered as a choice between different options to implement and enforce regulation. These approaches vary depending on the balance between the degree of governmental intervention and voluntary participation of the industry and include market-based solutions, self-regulation, co-regulation and statutory regulation [45: 5]. The most desirable solutions, which are referred to for the complex multi-stakeholder system of cybersecurity, are self-regulation and co-regulation as a compromise, which, on one hand, allows to avoid laissez-faire approach to the issues of the critical importance and, on the other hand, ensures that the development of the information technologies is not hampered by direct governmental intervention.

Though self-regulation and co-regulation by definition presume different levels of state intervention, there are various perceptions and practices within these two forms of regulation. Depending on the level of state involvement, two approaches to privatisation of regulation can be identified: top-down and bottom-up. Since co-regulation presumes the direct involvement of public actors in the regulatory process, especially with regard to enforcement, such regulatory mechanism is primarily considered or understood to take a "top-down" approach [46: 12] and to complement legislation rather than be an alternative to legal ordinances. On the contrary, self-regulation (at least in theory) is initiated by private stakeholders and established independently from the adoption of legal orders and, thus, follows a "bottom-up" approach [46: 12]. It should be noted, however, that even if self-regulation implies implementation and enforcement by private stakeholders themselves without the involvement of statutory obligations, this in fact often does not mean that the state stays away from the effort to impose self-regulation.

Both models exist in different jurisdictions. The co-regulatory approach as a strict form of collaboration happens when self-regulation involves public authority, reference in legislation or is introduced, overseen and/or enforced by the power of legal ordinance [47]. The degree of interference may vary from agreements between government and industry to the obligation of self-regulation imposed by law. In some cases, the lack of coordinated legal provisions can be the reason for co-regulation: in the Netherlands, co-regulatory procedures for taking down illegal content were implemented because the provisions of Criminal Code on ISP liability stipulate obligatory content removal, but no relevant procedure had been provided in legislation [48: 24].

The degree of softer government intervention in co-regulatory efforts may vary. It can take the form of support provided by government with regard to the creation of different organisations, associations and forums. The state can take part in the elaboration of agreements between the ISP associations and law enforcement agencies or provide support to the hotlines or reporting platforms carrying out awareness campaigns.

As distinct from co-regulation, which includes state participation and enforcement as a necessary component, self-regulation is represented by non-hierarchically organised private actors, such as industry associations and organisations that implement different mechanisms for self-regulation within the industry. The involvement of these actors in fighting cybercrime and providing cybersecurity varies from ad hoc collaboration upon police request to sustainable self-regulation, for example private hotlines for reporting illegal content. Many forms of self-regulation include the state either as initiator or participant, even when the enforcement of self-regulatory measures is assured by the private sector. It has often been asserted that the most successful cases of self-regulation involve some participation of the state in one form or another [49]. In contradiction to the perception of self-regulation as voluntary coordination, some studies argue that self-regulation could have a mandatory element, for example, by high-level statutory backing, or by self-regulatory bodies being specified in statute [47].

Despite the existence of different forms of self- and co-regulation, the current debate around private sector's involvement into cybersecurity is mostly revolving around public–private partnerships, which represent the distinct form of co-regulation. Two critical points should be made for the clarity of understanding of public–private collaboration in cybersecurity and cybercrime. First of all, the existing channels of collaboration, information sharing and other activities are much broader than the concept of public–private partnership and they have already more or less achieved the short- and medium-term goals of advancing the involvement of the private sector in cybersecurity. Secondly, the debate about public–private partnerships frequently gets this term misunderstood. Not every existing channel of collaboration and cooperation form, even if it is structured and sustainable, can be considered as a public–private "partnership". In theory, the ideal form of true partnership represents entities with "equivalent power over the relationship and at least somewhat differing goals and objectives agree to compromise their interests and jointly develop an action plan to achieve mutual gain for each other's objectives as well as mutual objectives" [50]. Any form of regulated self-regulation, mandatory reporting or even governmental coercion for regulated private entities to self-regulate certain areas would not be a partnership, but rather represent a form of direct governmental intervention. The scope of this book chapter goes beyond the debate on public–private partnerships and tries to analyse other valuable forms of collaboration, including ad hoc cases, to show the complexity of the issue and the degree of the involvement of the private sector.

Another misconception with regard to the forms of self- and co-regulation in cybersecurity is related to the choice of "bottom-up" versus "top-down" approaches. One of the examples is the so-called regulated self-regulation. For instance, in Germany the framework for self-regulation with regard to protecting minors online is established by the law that stipulates the duty of the self-control associations to make sure that their members act within the rules of the treaty for the protection of youth. Furthermore, several self-regulatory associations operating in Germany represent the case of "regulated self-regulation", a form of self-control that is initiated by the government: the state creates a framework for self-regulation and then gives the industry the leading role in developing the rules [23, 51]. Though being called with the use of the term "self-regulation", this form represents top-down approach with the direct intervention of the state to initiate safe regulation and to create a framework for it. The industry has no choice, even in the case if there are no other "incentives" than the state coercion.

Although self-regulation in theory shall be driven by market forces and the idea of resolving issues and advancing policy objectives without legislative intervention or a pressure from the state, it is hard, but not impossible, to find a pure example of bottom-up industry driven self-regulatory initiatives, which have not been at least to some extent informally encouraged by governments [31]. Despite the theoretical concept of top-down approach, governments can get involved in self-regulation indirectly, by approving the activity on one of the stages, or—even more tacit—by implementing legal provisions that lead to some forms of self-regulation and coordination within the industry. Publicly, debated legal frameworks and policy issues in the multi-stakeholder environment can help to set frameworks for self-regulation and co-regulation and encourage industry involvement [31: 14]. Thus, the need for self-regulation, though being "bottom-up" driven, in many cases still comes either as a result of statutory law supporting it or as a response to the indirect state coercion. When the government has no agenda for promoting and supporting self-regulation or does not implement legislation which would increase the willingness of the private sector to cooperate on cybersecurity, the private sector itself can be very sceptical about self-regulation or initiatives may be undermined by state apathy towards, lack of driving forces and uncertainty of, current legal statutes.

1.3.3 Legislating Cybersecurity?

The legal uncertainty of different regulatory domains related to various aspects of cybersecurity raises the question as to which legal frameworks should be used for regulation, be it direct governmental intervention or softer approaches such as self- and co-regulation. In this regard, distinction can be made between public–private collaboration in the field of tackling cybercrime and in the field of other cybersecurity concerns. Cybercrime always requires a strong involvement of public authorities [35: 2] because investigation and prosecution involves legal frameworks related to criminal and criminal procedural law. Any public–private collaboration represents an additional layer on the top of the frameworks providing direct governmental intervention. Criminal law is the sole domain of national governments and law enforcement agencies. This domain cannot and shall not be privatised. Thus, any cooperation between public authorities and private actors operates within the strict legal frameworks of criminal procedural law, international cooperation and jurisdiction. This, however, does not exclude a certain degree of flexibility with regard to prevention and detection of cybercrime—different self- and co-regulation initiatives, such as awareness raising campaigns, detection of malicious activity and takedown of botnets, can be added as another dimension of the efforts to tackle cybercrime.

Criminal law, however, though plays a very important role in securing safe online environment, cannot tackle the whole of complex of sophisticated threats related to critical information infrastructure procession and national security, because this field of law is meant to punish for severe breaches of the public order and not to identify relevant threats and develop an adequate response to them. The obvious need for collaboration and information sharing raised the question as to which extent such cooperation should be regulated and whether there is a need for an appropriate legislation. In this regard, the problem of bottom-up and top-down approaches becomes a very important issue for both industry and governments. This problem deepens due to the international dimension of cyber-threats: different approaches, which might be taken in various jurisdictions, can contribute to the possible fragmentation of the attempts to address the global problem of cybersecurity.

The problem of fragmentation has become very visible in the last couple of years with several attempts to legislate participation of the private sector in cybersecurity taken on both national and international level, which showed significant differences in the choice between statutory regulation and encouraging voluntary participation of the industry. The former approach has been chosen on the level of the European Union in the proposed draft of Network and Information Security (NIS) Directive, which introduced a far-reaching reporting obligations and mandatory information sharing in a form of direct regulation. According to the European Commission's proposal, the draft of the directive included critical information infrastructure operators and information society services into the scope of mandatory reporting and information sharing obligations. While EU Parliament excluded the latter from the draft, the current amendments proposed by the European Council brought back to the draft of the document not only the list of information society service oper-ators proposed by the European Commission, such as cloud service providers and social networking websites, but also suggested to include national domain name registries and web-hosting platforms. At the same time, European Council proposed a clause that the decision on which entities are to be included into the obligatory reporting of security breaches should be taken by the member states. There are also attempts to regulate cybersecurity on the national level taken by some of the EU countries. For example, Germany in its draft of the IT security law introduced several new obligations, in addition to reporting obligations for the critical infra-structure operators.

The above-mentioned attempts represent clear top-down approach to the partici-pation of private sector in cybersecurity. A contrary way to legislate cybersecurity is adoption of the laws that are framing public–private collaboration and trying to provide incentives for the private sector to participate in joint efforts. One of the examples of such legislation is the Cybersecurity Directive and Executive order in the USA. Adopted in 2013–2014, this approach implements encouraging instead of coercion and tries to provide incentives for reporting and information sharing.

The notion behind toughening the regulation in cybersecurity is the idea that the interests of private and public partners are not matching, and the private sector is not interested in providing the level of cybersecurity that would be enough for the nation and society, and, thus, shall be regulated. There are several possible regu-latory approaches emerging as a response to the "unwillingness" of private sector to collaborate. One of them is pure top-down regulation with strict duties and liabil-ities. Another one is softer, but still represents a top-down model: regulated self-regulation. The degree of the latter may vary from self-regulation codes developed by the governments, when all the industry players are forced to follow the obli-gations established by these documents, or mandatory frameworks for the industry. The problem of shifting regulatory landscape and the drawbacks of the attempts to legislate cybersecurity will be further discussed in the Sect. 1.5, after the overview of current initiatives which go far beyond the concepts of public–private partner-ships and include the constantly evolving forms of public–private collaboration.

1.4 Existing Initiatives: From Illegal Content Towards Cyber-Resilience

The development of cybersecurity policy went from the task of fighting cybercrime to the complex of solutions involving proactive and holistic approaches. However, the evolvement of public–private collaboration started with the cooperation related to tackling cybercrime. As it will be further analysed in the Chap. 2 of this book, first initiatives, back to the 1990s, included mainly cooperation for taking down illegal content and reporting online child abuse. Successful establishment of private hotlines for reporting illegal content together with further development of information technologies has been driving the new concept of public–private collaboration in fighting cybercrime in a multi-stakeholder environment. Growing dependency on information technologies and new threats, such as botnets, decentralised services (cloud computing), phishing and sophistication of social engineering techniques for committing online frauds called for further participation of different intermediaries in the process of securing a safe cyberspace. Industry and Internet intermediaries in this context became a growing focal point for Internet policy on national and, later, on international levels [31: 9]. Nowadays, the scope and scale of public–private collaboration in fighting cybercrime and providing cybersecurity goes far beyond illegal content issues and involves different areas of ICT markets and various forms of cooperation: from ad hoc to long-term public–private partnerships and nationwide joint cybersecurity initiatives.

1.4.1 Fighting Cybercrime: Forms of Cooperation

1.4.1.1 Hotlines and Reporting Platforms—The First Forms of Collaboration

One of the first types of collaboration between the private sector and governments in fighting cybercrime was private reporting platforms and hotlines established in the 1990s. In particular, the first hotlines for reporting illegal content were promoted by the European Union Action Plan and the UK's Internet Watch Foundation (IWF). The IWF—a private industry-based self-regulatory body—runs as a hotline for reporting online child abuse content. It was announced in September 1996 with the support of the UK government as a private body supported financially by the ISPs [52: p. 307]. Another example of public–private collaboration in this field is the pan-European hotline association INHOPE, formed in 1999 and expanding rapidly in Europe in the beginning of the 2000s. Funded by Safer Internet Action Plan and Microsoft, this association aims to coordinate and build capacity in reporting illegal content [49]. The development of this form of collaboration is analysed in the Chap. 2 in detail.

1.4.1.2 Industry Codes of Conducts

Another form of self- and co-regulation is codes of conduct (or codes of practices) on cybersecurity and cybercrime, which have been adopted in many states. These codes of practice set rules on behaviour of the private industry players in particular circumstances: respect for privacy, protection of minors and application of filtering software. The most common form with regard to addressing cybercrime is the ISPs' codes of conduct, for example, notice-and-takedown code of conduct in the Netherlands, "Voluntary self-control of multimedia providers" that forbids providing access to illegal content (e.g. pornography or content that is harmful for minors), Australian ISP code of practice on cybersecurity.

1.4.1.3 Public Awareness Campaigns

Furthermore, government and private industry can cooperate on raising public awareness on cybersecurity and cybercrime. One of the examples of such collaboration is the "Stay Safe Online" project of the National Security Alliance in the USA, which was launched in 2010 as a public awareness campaign in partnership between the US Department of Homeland Security, the Federal Trade Commission and private industry [53: 27]. Such awareness campaigns might be directed either on situational awareness (for example, to the mitigation of a particular cybersecurity threat or introduction of cybersecurity measures) or long-term educational programmes aiming to build and sustain end-users' knowledge on how to protect themselves online [54].

1.4.1.4 Education and Capacity Building

The knowledge and expertise of private industry can significantly benefit governments through educational and capacity-building programmes for law enforcement agencies. Some successful initiatives, such as International Centre for Missing and Exploited Children, provide training programmes for police officers and prosecutors around the world to fight online child abuse. Under this initiative, Microsoft and the International Centre for Missing and Exploited Children are cooperating with more than 30 financial institutions worldwide, including credit-card companies, to establish a system that can detect online commercial transactions involving offences against children [55: 94]. Another successful capacity-building initiative is the 2Centre project established in 2010 and supported by Microsoft and the European Commission. 2Centre represents cooperation between law enforcement agencies, industry and academia to deliver training to key cybercrime personnel.

1.4.1.5 Ad hoc Collaboration and Call for Structured Approaches

Many contacts with private parties in fighting cybercrime are made on a case-by-case basis rather than by memoranda of understanding [29: 38]. Such cases of ad hoc private–public collaboration include, for example, the so-called Mikado operation carried out in Germany in 2006. In 2004, a German TV station had identified a website offering the download of child pornography with payments via Internet credit-card transaction into a specific account. Twenty-two German credit-card firms were asked to scan all their clients' credit-card transactions from 2004 and identify those clients who had transferred specific amounts of money into the accounts of criminals. The cooperation with banks took place on a voluntary basis, and transactions on millions of credit cards were checked without the consent of their owners. This led to the identification of more than 300 persons who had purchased child-abuse material [56: p. 16]. Ad hoc collaboration can also be carried out on the international level: for example, cooperation between the American, Moroccan and Turkish police, and Microsoft led to the arrests of the developers and distributors of the Zotob Virus [57, 58].

1.4.2 Cybersecurity: A Call for More Structured Approaches

The raise of the cybersecurity issues on the top of political agenda and the urgent need to address a complex set of threats put a significant pressure on both governments and, as a result, on private parties to build new forms of cooperation which were, as it is characterised by Thomas [59], mostly "built upon pre-existing relationships, historical connections and organisational structures originally intended for other purposes in fashioning the first generation of cybersecurity PPPs—yielding structures that often reflect expedience rather than thoughtful design".

1.4.2.1 Urgent Response: Ah hoc Collaboration

The millennium software bug was already mentioned as a turning point for widening the scope of security initiatives from reactively addressing the problems of cybercrime to the development of the concept of cybersecurity. In this regard, Lewis [27] refers to the response to "Year 2000 Problem" (Y2K) as to a first new approach to addressing public problem of information security. Though the potential threat turned out to be exaggerated, the way to solve it gave a promise of new cooperative models, where governments and private industry combine their efforts in addressing the potential vulnerability of the information networks. The approach to Y2K was twofold and represented a combination of voluntary cooperation and coercion: on one hand, it involved government's efforts to collaborate voluntary and educate users and businesses about the problem; on the other hand, the government was exercising its mandate through Securities and Exchange Commission (SEC) regulations and made the private industry to report on the efforts they made to respond to the threat [27].

Another notable effort of voluntary collaboration—Confiker working group—was also born out of the sense of urgency to address the problem of vulnerabilities. The threat posed by sophisticated botnet worm Confiker, which infected millions of computers all around the world, forced representatives from the industry, academia and non-profit organisations to form a working group which managed to stop the spread of the worm. Interestingly, the participation of the governments in this working group was based on the concept of equal footing: they were not initiating the efforts and did not take any leading role there [18]. This group, again, represents an ad hoc collaboration, which successfully addressed the problem and was dismissed after the solution was found.

Such ad hoc initiatives together with the experience of cooperation gained from tackling the problem of cybercrime to a certain extent proved the ability of public and private parties to collaborate at least on ad hoc basis to address the urgent problems. Later, the need for a structured approach [29: 38] created more sophisticated and cross-sector forms of alliances, especially in mitigating cybersecurity threats, critical information infrastructure protection and investigating cybercrime, which were created to serve long-term goals. One of the examples of such collaboration in many countries was creation of CERTs, which in many countries represent a teamwork involving academia, governments and private sector.

1.4.2.2 Towards Long-term Collaboration and Structured Approaches

One of the first attempts to establish and frame long-term collaboration structures was an "unprecedented" [60: 226] public–private agreement between Google and the National Security Agency where Google was seeking to benefit from the NSA's expertise in evaluating the vulnerabilities in its hardware and software and get a better understanding on system penetration and, in turn, offers to share with the NSA any data about the nature of the harmful codes that were used by intruders [61: 1–2].

The first successful long-term initiatives in cybersecurity were represented by government-industry botnet mitigation agreements, which became one of the main tools for tackling the problem of malicious software. Since ISPs have been recognised as a critical point in botnet detection, several countries involved intermediaries or their associations in ongoing malware and botnet mitigation programmes. These programmes include such projects as:

- Japanese Cyber Clean Centre project [31: 114];
- A partnership of German ISPs (led by Eco) and the BSI Bot-Frei, which detects and notifies infected customers and provides assistance to clean users' computers;
- Anti-botnet treaty in the Netherlands which represents a partnership of 14 Dutch ISPs and the Telecom Regulatory Authority (OPTA) covering 98 % of the Dutch market;
- Botnet MoU project in Denmark: a cooperation framework between ISPs and CERTs [62] and many others.

The threat of malware and botnets and the perceived success of the national projects on botnet mitigation on the national level encouraged ENISA to include botnet mitigation to the agenda of the European Public Private Partnership for Resilience—EP3R [63]. This partnership actually was one of the first attempts to establish cross-national partnerships in the area of cybersecurity and was initially considered as a very promising initiative. However, its performance up to now has very mixed reviews. Robinson [37] highlights two major challenges. Firstly, there was no clarity with the mandate on the EU body that should be facilitating the partnership. Secondly, EP3R has failed to understand the incentives of stakeholder and encourage them to participate. Irion [32] criticises the lack of engagement in information sharing and exchange, which could have become a motivation for private actors to participate, the concept of "trusted participation" limiting involvement to senior representatives and the lack of transparency and accountability.

Analysis of factors that caused the failure of EP3R can definitely contribute to learning lessons and avoiding repetition of the same mistakes in future initiatives. International strategic alliances between public and private parties would inevitably be the next necessary step to fight cybercrime and maintain cybersecurity, since many of the critical infrastructure sectors are privately owned and dependency on information technologies grows not only on the national but also on the international level. The benefits from such alliances can include increased reporting of the incidents to police, effective and timely information sharing, efficient work with digital evidence in cross-border investigations, reduced costs, avoidance of effort duplication and better capacity building for law enforcement agencies [55: p. 95].

1.4.2.3   Cybersecurity: National Initiatives and Projects

The possible way forward for creation of international anti-cybercrime public–private partnerships is to adopt the best practices from wide-national cybersecurity initiatives that have been developed in some states. For example, the Netherlands carried out a project, "National infrastructure against cybercrime", which implied joint public–private assessment of cybersecurity measures and included Cybercrime Reporting Unit, the High Tech Crime Team of the National Police Services Agency, National Alerting Service, the government's Computer Emergency Response Team and cross-industry stakeholders running critical infrastructure. The initiative consists of various components covering a broad spectrum of measures to fight cybercrime and sustain cybersecurity: a contact point, reporting unit, trend watching, monitoring and detection, information distribution, education, warning, development, knowledge sharing, surveillance, prevention, termination and mitigation. In 2012, the Netherlands set up a new platform for public–private collaboration, namely National Cyber Security Centre (NCSC) to improve the coordination among different agencies and stakeholders involved in fighting online crime [64]. The centre aims at focusing on developing and offering expertise and advice, supporting and implementing responses to threats or incidents and strengthening crisis management [65].

Another project focusing on broader public–private collaboration has been established in Australia, where the government launched the Cyber Security Operations Centre in collaboration with AusCERT and Trusted Information Sharing Network for Critical Infrastructure Protection (TISN). Under the umbrella of the TISN, CERT Australia operates the three sectoral exchanges to share technical information in the banking sector, communication sectors and owners and operators of control systems in power and water utilities [66].

These national cross-sector collaboration programmes can be a starting point for future consideration. Best practices of establishing, enforcing and maintaining collaboration between public and private parties towards different sectors can be leveraged on the international level. Other examples of the national initiatives include different partnerships, both sector-specific and cross-sector:

- Swiss Reporting and Analysis Centre for Information Assurance (MELANI), which represents collaborative attempt to secure computer systems of businesses and individual users and protection of critical national infrastructures.
- The Centre for the Protection of National Infrastructure (CPNI) in the UK, which aims to protect national security by providing protective security advice and has relationships with private and public sector partners such as National Technical Authority for Information Assurance, National Counter Terrorism Security Office and the Counter Terrorism Security Advisor network.
- A sectorial initiative in Austria project "Cybersecurity ICT—Risk Assessment of the Austrian Power Sector", which involved public and private sectors and a national regulatory authority, was based on voluntary participation. The project aimed to assess the cybersecurity risks and develop possible solution and, after successful completion, was extended to the gas sector and developed a set of new aims such as implement recommendations and exchange the knowledge with international partners.
- Cyber Security Coalition in Belgium is recently (October, 2014) launched by the partners from three sectors. The initial aim of the coalition is to bring together more than 50 key players from the academic world, the business sector and the public authorities to share knowledge and experiences and jointly obtain an overall picture of the cybersecurity landscape.

1.5 Problems and a Way Forward

Many of the existing collaborative initiatives in the field of cybersecurity and cybercrime emerged from an ad hoc urgency and the necessity to solve current problems. These models did not have time and capacity for analysis of the best suitable structures and development of systematic approaches. Thomas [59] points out that some of the public–private partnerships achieved success "in spite of perceived flaws in partnership design and governance". In the past few years, public–private collaboration based on voluntary (or at least they were referred to as "voluntary") approaches have been criticised in the literature due to different factors. Mostly, critiques of the public–private partnerships in the field of cybersecurity mention the unwillingness of the private sector to collaborate, lack of incentives and clear strategies, badly defined goals and objectives, non-matching interests of public and private partners and limitations of enforcement and inability to produce an optimal outcome [27, 32, 67, 68].

Due to the growing concerns related to catastrophic scenarios of possible cybersecurity apocalypses on one hand, and perceived failure of collaboration models especially in the form of public–private partnerships on the other hand, strong voices for a tougher governmental intervention have been raised both in the academic literature and among legislators. As it was discussed in this chapter, the misunderstanding of the terms "cybercrime" and "national security" leads to the adoption of cybersecurity strategies that propose tougher regulation for both sectors without understanding that existing channels of collaboration differ and so do the legal frameworks for different domains.

1.5.1 Limitations: Mandate of the Governments in Criminal Law and Security

Public–private collaboration is not a flawless solution. It has its limitations, especially in the field of detecting, investigating and prosecuting cybercrime. Due to the unique mandate of the government and the nature of criminal law, public–private collaboration in the investigation or prevention serves the purpose to attribute or avert criminal acts, but it can never substitute proper legal frameworks. First of all, the power to enforce rules in the field of criminal law is limited to the governments and has to follow very strict safeguards and procedures, because of the human rights component involved in the criminal investigations. Thus, any approaches for collaboration, be they ad hoc or structured, should operate within strict rules protecting the rights of suspects, victims and any other citizens and entities which might be affected by criminal investigations. Any self-regulatory initiatives have to be built upon those legal frameworks. Secondly, the existence of public–private collaboration cannot alone guarantee appropriate investigation of the crime and prosecution of offenders. For example, the agreements or codes of conduct adopted by industry cannot completely prevent or eliminate certain forms of cybercrime, such as the distribution of child pornography. Moreover, in the absence of proper cybercrime legislation and procedural frameworks for investigation, offenders can easily circumvent industry codes of conducts due to transnational nature of cybercrime [36].

Another constraint related to cybercrime is the conflict between cross-border nature of the Internet and the sovereignty issues. Criminal law is a domain of the nation state and despite the necessity for harmonisation of criminal law and procedural frameworks and collaboration both between law enforcement agencies in different countries and law enforcement and private industry, the investigation and prosecution of cybercrime is solely a duty and responsibility of the nation state [11]. This is why some sensitive matters such as human rights, bulk collection of information, transfer of communication data between ISPs and law enforcement agencies are usually discussed on the level of the nation state. In this regard, frameworks for collaboration which go beyond investigation and prosecution of cybercrime have fewer limitations because of the absence of strict legal borders determined by criminal law and, thus, can be more flexible.

1.5.2 Degree of Governmental Intervention

The challenge posed by the unique mandate of the governments brings the next issue, namely the degree of governmental intervention, which is necessary to achieve security and policy objectives. Again, the situation differs for cybercrime and national security (including information infrastructure protection). In the case of cybercrime, many countries have already adopted legal frameworks in the area of criminal law and criminal procedure law, so the problem here is not to legislate, but to, first of all, make the existing frameworks operable and, secondly, build the sustainable channels of collaboration between governments and industry. In the case of cybercrime, it is very hard to avoid regulation and intervention, especially when human rights component is concerned, such as in the case of freedom of speech protection and in the case of illegal content takedown, enforced data retention, production order, disclosure of traffic data, interception capabilities, just to name a few. Strict frameworks do not leave much room for flexibility in investigations, so public–private collaboration with "voluntary" element is usually directed on training, awareness, quick channels for handling information, better procedures for safeguards and human rights and customer care.

A very different picture can be seen in the field of national security and CIIP where mostly hands-off approaches were common till recently. In the last few years, there have been attempts to legislate cybersecurity and to adopt frameworks aiming to build "better" or more structured approaches to public–private collaboration in this field. Most of those initiatives deal with information sharing and incident reporting obligations. There is, however, a growing concern that some of the new policy and legislation initiatives, such as EU NIS directive, may aim to replace collaborative models with those reliant on tough regulation exercised by governments and coercing industry.

The best analogy for describing the proposals for tough regulation and coercing is made by Clinton [69: p. 103] and is worth to be quoted in full[3]:

> … this type of relationship would be like one spouse saying to the other, "Honey, your job is going to be to do all the things necessary to secure our family. You will have to generate the money, buy the house, clean the house, pay the bills, buy the food, cook the dinner, have the kids, raise the kids, etc. My job will be to evaluate how well you do your job. And, of course, if you don't meet my specifications, there will be severe penalties." The partnership described in this construction is similar to a parent–child relationship, wherein the parent (government) feels the need to exhibit some tough love on an uncooperative and immature child (the private sector).
>
> The analogy breaks down, however, when one realizes that in this case the "child" (industry) is actually far bigger, stronger, and has more resources than the supposed parent. Indeed, it is the parent (government) in this case that is ultimately reliant on the child for cyber security.

---

[3]The excerpt from the article "A Relationship on the Rocks: Industry-Government Partnership for Cyber Defense" written by Larry Clinton and published in the Journal of Strategic Security 4, no. 2 (2011): 97–112 is quoted with a kind permission of the Journal of Strategic Security.

It is understandable that the governments are under the pressure to "do something", and since regulation and coercion are the tools that many governments are used to rely on, implementation of mandatory requirements seems to be an obvious way (and much easier one compare to a long path of building mutual trust and confidence) to force industry to provide an adequate level cybersecurity. This change, however, is more than a shift in choice of the tougher regulatory approach. Many efforts have been taken to build public–private collaboration so far, and implementation of tough regulation and pure coercion might undermine all the efforts [70].

Another problem is misunderstanding with regard to regulatory mandates. The call for tougher regulation on public–private collaboration in cybersecurity usually refers to cybercrime. However, due to the different rules and channels and activities for collaboration, what is working in cybercrime will not work for cybersecurity and vice versa. Governments, instead of taking into account already existing mechanisms, opt for regulated self-regulation and prefer to establish their own private sector entities that are supposed to run collaboration programs, leaving the private sector with no choice but work with these organisations [50]. Clinton [50] refers to these kinds of organisation as to "setting up the parallel universe" and suggests leveraging the core competences of existing organisation which have long-established links with the industry, such as industry associations, instead of competing with them.

It is clear that some of the initiatives rather go to the direction of regulation and try to force the industry to "collaborate" such as the EU Cybersecurity Strategy. Further efforts are now being made to toughen regulation and it is not clear which version of it will be passed yet, to adopt of the EU NIS directive. The draft of the NIS directive and all the debates around it represent a good case to illustrate how the concepts of regulation, self-regulation and co-regulation can get confused when it comes to mandate of the governments and collaboration between public and private sectors.

1.5.3 EU NIS Directive: From Voluntary Collaboration to Statutory Regulation?

EU NIS directive introduced mandatory reporting obligations of security incidents instead of voluntary collaboration. These reporting obligations cover a wide range of information society services and critical information infrastructure operators. The scope of this requirement has been criticised as unprecedented and unnecessary broad [37, 71]. The list of market operators included information society services that have never been regulated before. Annex II of the proposed directive included the following list of market operators:

- e-commerce platforms
- Internet payment gateways

- Social networks
- Search engines
- Cloud computing services
- Application stores.

The inclusion of information society services was fiercely discussed on the national and international level with regard to the vagueness of the definition of the market players, ambiguity of the reporting obligation and unprecedented shifting of approaches from encouraging voluntary cooperation to statutory regulation. As a result of these discussions, in March 2014, the EU Parliament excluded the information society services from the scope of the proposed directive.[4] However, later in October 2014, the debate around the scope of the obligation moved to the level of the Council of the European Union, which not only added all the information society services excluded by the European Parliament but also extended the list of information society services by including Internet exchange points, national domain name registries and web-hosting services [72]. In addition, due to the lack of consensus with regard to which entities should be a subject of the reporting obligation, the Council of the European Union proposed to leave to the national governments' power to define the scope of the reporting obligation by identifying entities that meet the definition of operators.[5]

Some of the EU member states discuss similar regulations even ahead of the adoption of the EU NIS directive. The most notable example in this regard is the German draft of IT security law, which is partially based on the same proposal as that made in the EU NIS draft Directive: it imposes security obligation and requires incident notification. In some parts, however, it goes even further than the EU proposal and introduces a set of new obligations, increasing the regulatory burden for telecommunication providers and information society services (Telemedien).

---

[4]See Amendment 132, European Parliament legislative resolution of 13 March 2014 on the proposal for a directive of the European Parliament and of the Council concerning measures to ensure a high common level of network and information security across the Union [COM(2013)0048—C7-0035/2013—2013/0027(COD)].

[5]The text of amendment proposed by the European Council: Art. 3(8) "operator" means a public or private entity referred to in Annex II, which provides an essential service in the fields of infrastructure enabling the provision of information society services, energy, transport, banking, financial markets, health and water supply and which fulfils all of the following criteria:

- the service depends heavily on network and information systems;
- an incident to the network and information systems of the service having serious disruptive effects for critical social and economic activities [and/]or having [serious] public safety implications.

"Each Member State shall identify on its territory entities, which meet the above definition of operator." Council of the European Union [72].

Telecommunication providers, in addition to the reporting obligations, have to[6]:

- notify the Federal Network Agency in case of the impairment of telecommunication networks and services which can lead to significant security violations or unauthorised access to telecommunication and data processing systems of the end-users;
- inform affected subscribers/users if the providers become aware of impairments which originate from the users' data processing systems (such as malware) and in addition, provide information about appropriate, effective and accessible technical means allowing those subscribers/users to discover and remove such impairments.

Furthermore, commercial information society services are obliged to:

- implement technical and organisational measures to generally protect the telecommunication and data processing systems against unauthorised access;
- offer a reasonably secure authentication procedure in case of personalised services.

The outcome of the bill is still unknown, because the draft is currently being debated. It is very likely, however, that the Bill will be passed, even despite the concerns affected private entities raised with regard to the new regulatory burden [74].

The overview of the recent discussions in the EU represents just a snapshot of the current state of an ongoing debate on the legislating cybersecurity and choosing between bottom-up and top-down approaches. At the moment when this chapter was being written, the outcome of the debate is still uncertain. Both EU NIS directive and the draft of the German IT security law might undergo a set of changes and get passed in different versions. However, what is currently happening highlights several critical problems of self- and co-regulatory approaches in cybersecurity that might have significant impact on the future collaboration in this field.

The first problem is the whole concept of "collaboration" and "public–private partnership". Though the current channels of cooperation have been created as a response to urgency, though there is luck of the structured approaches, existing forms of collaboration have been constantly evolving and gaining certain reliability. Imposing the new regulatory scheme, which by the means of statutory regulation forces private industry to "collaborate", means disregarding all existing efforts and already trusted channels.

Furthermore, attempts to turn to the use of coercion raise the questions of trust and enforceability of the obligations. Cybersecurity is rather a concept or a process, than a result, and trust in relationship between the governments and a private industry is an intangible issue that cannot be enforced or imposed by just simply implementing mandatory obligations for sharing information about threats. Thus, one of the drawbacks of the top-down approaches is the possible lack of trust and lack of opportunities to build it. The Council of the European Union refers to the debates among EU members with highlighting this issue [72: 3]:

---

[6]The translation of the German IT security Draft law is cited from Kuschewsky [73].

...some delegations point to the fruitful experience gained on the basis of voluntary notification and argue that trust cannot be imposed whereas others, on the other hand, believe that the Directive should result in firm commitments as well as allow for the building of confidence and trust over time

The current debate about trust and commitment both on the national and international level resembles chicken and egg issue. The answer as to what comes first—trust or commitments—to a large degree is influenced by the current state of voluntary collaboration in the particular country. The governments are pressured to do something and some of them believe that structured approaches and regulation might create the trust with time. However, this is a dangerous approach with regard to the whole "partnership" concept, because it excludes voluntary element and puts pressure—probably, on those private entities, which already do something [37: 19].

Furthermore, regulation of information society services is unprecedented. Many of the information society services have already become a part of voluntary collaboration. The new regulation can disregard existing channels (or even destroy them) and create unnecessary regulatory burden.

Another pitfall of the NIS directive regulatory model is the differences concerning the international component and the global nature of cybersecurity problem. For example, in the USA, despite several attempts to adopt more strict regulation[7] [75], recently adopted cybersecurity legislation[8] takes different approach and tries to create incentives for voluntary cooperation. Thus, with the adoption of the EU NIS directive, the USA and European Union member states can experience significant differences in their approaches to global problems, which require rather consistency, harmonisation and collaboration [76: 5, 77]. Further fragmentation of approaches to public–private collaboration might happen if the EU will pass a directive with the clause that each country can decide which entities fall under mandatory reporting as it has been proposed by the Council of the European Union. The general disagreement on governmental intervention among the EU member states is already clear on the stage of debating the scope of the directive. It is very likely that when it comes to implementation on the national level, not only the main goal of the directive—harmonisation of the policies and strategies and creation of the pan-European approach to NIS—will not be achieved, but the outcome might be a patchwork of incompatible policy and regulatory approaches which will create compliance challenges for the multinational entities or global services providers operating in different jurisdictions.

---

[7]e.g. Protecting cyberspace as a National Asset Act of 2010, Cybersecurity Act of 2010, Cybersecurity Act of 2012; for more information see [75].

[8]Presidential Executive Order 2013 and a Cybersecurity Framework 2014 issued by the National Institute for Standards and Technology.

1.5.4 Safeguards

Other likely risks associated with public–private partnerships, especially those in investigating cybercrime, include the negligent creation of opportunities for corruption, mishandling of investigations, loss or lack of confidence and transparency [55: 95]. Ahlert et al. [78] also raised a particular issue of the transparency and accountability of the notice-and-takedown procedures, arguing that content removal can take a form of private censorship with no limits upon the judgements of the private party. Other frequently discussed problems are the deficit of control, limitation of enforcement in cross-border environment [79: 52], privacy concerns and lack of mechanisms to protect the rights of individuals when the private parties are empowered to regulate and enforce regulation.

The transparency and accountability problems are inevitable due to the complexity of the ecosystem and large and diverse number of state and non-state actors involved in cybersecurity, which cuts across mandates of different governmental bodies (e.g. criminal justice, armed force, national security) and also legal and technical complexity of cybersecurity field [80: 18–19]. Furthermore, the oversight of the collaboration on the national level can fail when it extends across the borders or beyond the mandate of the particular regulator on the national level [80: 18–19].

Another issue emerging as a result of sensationalisation of the concept of cybersecurity and prioritisation of cybersecurity above any other issues is human rights and safeguards. This problem arises from the focus of debate on security, where security issues dominate over discussions on civil right and liberties and administrative actors getting more and more central role in establishing security policy, for example in the EU [11].

Though some studies argue that collaborative models for cybersecurity have more advantages such as privacy and civil liberties because they leave "network monitoring responsibilities for private networks where they belong—with the private sector operators—rather than having governmental agencies monitor those networks" (Center for democracy and technology: 7), which promotes transparency for addressing the civil liberty issues publicly. While this argument can certainly be relevant concerning transparency and accountability, the problem that needs to be addressed is still the implementation of the proper safeguards when bulk data are collected and monitored and protection of personal data when the information is shared. This problem has another dimension with regard to cybercrime investigation and prevention collaboration, because of the blurring borders of different legal regimes. The shift from reactive to proactive approach in policing cybercrimes is especially dangerous in terms of human rights and safeguards [8]. The data can be collected in the absence of suspicion or private industry that can be actively participating in monitoring data and traffic. While in criminal investigations, this can be solved by implementing strict safeguards concerning procedural law frameworks, and in the area of cybersecurity and information sharing and prevention and early disruption, the absence of clear safeguards in now combined with the bulk collection and monitoring. This can impede the privacy rights of millions of Internet users. The possibility of such sharing is stressed in the study of the European Parliament on National Programmes for mass surveillance of personal data in EU member states [81]. The study refers to the testimony of the Europol Director Rob Wainwright, who admitted during the European Parliament hearing that the data got by the Europol agents might possibly come from different sources including intelligence agencies of the EU member states and from outside the EU, such as NSA [81: 37]. In this regard, collection of data only from lawful sources and by lawful means as well as implementation of human rights safeguards and data protection measures should be one of the top priorities for public–private collaboration, especially when sensitive information is shared in the absence of suspicion or for the aim of prevention of cybersecurity incidents.

1.5.5 Incentives and Costs

Other problems arise from the necessity to implement self-regulatory measures on a cost-effective basis. For example, in Germany, the efforts of some ISPs to establish an age-verification system were undermined by the lack of international standards, the complexity of the procedure and the lack of coordination within the industry: customers may easily switch to the ISP that does not implement age-verification measures [51]. The lack of resources and industry incentives to implement self-regulation was reported in New Zealand, where the attitude among the industry towards voluntary obligations is to consider them a burden rather than a cost-effective solution [82]. The cost issue has also been among the main problems in the USA, where the government relies on public–private partnerships in maintaining cybersecurity, while commercial organisations might see computer security as a cost and do not value the corresponding benefits [83].

A cost-effective solution in this sense is one of the key points to get industry involved: while cybersecurity initiative presumes that industry should have the discretion to step up such efforts, this is not self-evident, because the market is first and foremost driven by price, and even if consumers or governments care about security, there might be lack of adequate market signals for all interested parties: consumers, industry and government [84].

Though successful cases of self-regulation and co-regulation in tackling the problem of cybercrime can be witnessed in many states, there are still problems with regard to the promotion, implementation and enforcement of these measures and also concerning the structural approaches and clear frameworks. Moreover, the economic complexity of cyberspace infrastructure makes it hard to manage public–private initiatives in fighting cybercrime [55: 95].

1.5.6 Way Forward: Is Statutory Regulation Still an Option?

Summing up, self-regulation is most likely to be effective when there is a collective interest among the industry stakeholders to solve particular issues and trust between public and private partners; private players are capable of defining clear objectives and frameworks for co- or self-regulatory schemes; the likely solution meets legitimate consumer and citizen expectations; the rules are enforceable either privately or with the support of the government [31: 14]. Development of public–private partnerships can be seriously hampered by the lack of any of those criteria. Lack of interest among industry and the absence of coordinated initiatives or government support will hold the developments back even in case of increasing concerns on Internet safety among private stakeholders. Passiveness of any of the two parties, public or private, will have the same effect.

It is also very important to understand what public–private "collaboration" actually means and where is the border between self- and co-regulation and direct governmental intervention. No government can expect "pure" bottom-up approaches in the complex environment. In contrast, "voluntary" does not always mean coming from the industry without any governmental participation. The true collaboration requires efforts and financial contributions from both parties. Thus, before the public sector has not tried to provide incentives, financial assistance, not attempted to build trust though encouraging the existing channels and developing the new approaches, it cannot be said that self- and co-regulation have failed to meet expectations. There is a need to learn from both successful and unsuccessful models of cooperation, including those which failed to add real value to the goal of securing cyberspace, or those which were lacking transparency, or did not have enough support from either governments or private sector, which were not open and inclusive. Implementation of the strong statutory regulation with the compliance requirements under "one-size-fits-all" approach, demanding commitments from the industry, might seem the easier way compared to the long path of building trust and learning from the mistakes. However, the rapidly evolving cybersecurity threats require quick reaction and adaptation from the industry, in which strict requirements for regulatory compliance might possibly hamper, and instead of achieving a greater level of cybersecurity, the statutory regulation might in the longer perspective decrease it.

1.6 Conclusion

Government intervention and voluntary approaches in the field of cybersecurity are not mutually exclusive. The dichotomy "hands-off approach versus statutory regulation", which is frequently discussed in the context of cybersecurity, is rather confusing and misleading: cybersecurity requires a combination of strict legal frameworks of criminal law and criminal procedure, safeguards and data protection measures with a careful hands-off approach and trust-building measures when it comes to identifying quickly evolving threats, sharing information and developing an adequate response. Apparently, finding the right balance in the complex eco-system is hard due to the myriads of stakeholders involved, different areas of regulatory domains and fast-evolving cyber-threats. However, cybersecurity is both a concept and a process, which are hard to be measured adequately. There would be no ideal "state" of cybersecurity—while information technologies are evolving, existence of these technologies and their vulnerable and transborder nature are the primary factors for the evolvement of cybercrime and cyber-threats. Thus, the process of identifying the new threats, predicting and mitigating the risks would always be a part of the cybersecurity efforts, since there is no silver bullet solution to stop infringements in cyberspace once and forever.

As a part of the collaborative efforts, self- and co-regulation in the last two decades have become an essential part of national and international strategies to fight cybercrime and maintain cybersecurity. Both governments and private stakeholders mutually benefited from joint efforts to secure overall community threat prevention and better understand the interests of each other [85: 10]. Involvement of the industry, be it voluntary or with a shadow of the state in the form of self- or co-regulation, is being achieved at the national level in many countries. This involvement has gone far beyond the first form of cooperation such as ad hoc collaboration for investigating particular cases of cybercrime or blocking and removing illegal content. Co- and self-regulation have taken the forms of industry cybercrime codes of conduct, public–private reporting platforms, multi-industry public–private collaboration programmes against cybercrime, national botnet detection and mitigation projects involving ISPs, just to name a few.

With all the substantial efforts that have already been taken in building solutions for co- and self-regulation in fighting cybercrime and addressing cybersecurity threats, the shift from supporting voluntary approaches to the state coercion and mandatory security obligations disregards the trust and capacity that have been built in the last decade. Instead of taking a possibly counterproductive step, it would be better to enhance the effectiveness of the existing models and build upon them. Like any relationship between partners, public–private collaboration encounters problems; however, changing the whole partnership paradigm to command-and-control model is not the right solution. Instead, the efforts should be directed to developing coordinated approach, providing efficient government support, promoting inclusiveness and finding cost-effective solutions. The key issue for governments is to raise interest among private industry and to find incentives for co- and self-regulation. Though pure self-regulation shall ideally follow a "bottom-up" approach, there is still a need for promoting these measures, encouraging private actors to take voluntary obligations in order to address cybersecurity problem. At the same time, harmonisation of efforts to promote self- and co-regulation needs to be coordinated at an international level to avoid fragmentation of approaches to a truly transnational problem of cybersecurity.

References

1. Nye J (2010) Cyberpower. Belfer center for science and international affairs, Harvard Kennedy School, May 2010 [Online]. Available at: http://belfercenter.ksg.harvard.edu/files/cyber-power.pdf
2. Barrett et al (2011) Combating cybercrime. Principles, Policies, and Programs. April 2011, PayPal [Online]. Available at: https://www.paypal-media.com/assets/pdf/fact_sheet/PayPal_CombatingCybercrime_WP_0411_v4.pdf
3. Finklea K, Theohary C (2013) Cybercrime: conceptual issues for congress and U.S. law enforcement [Online]. Available at: https://www.fas.org/sgp/crs/misc/R42547.pdf
4. Hathaway O et al (2012) The law of cyber-attack. California Law Rev100(4), 2012; Yale Law and economics research paper no. 453; Yale Law School, public law working paper no. 258. Available at SSRN: http://ssrn.com/abstract=2134932
5. Cornish P et al (2010) On cyber warfare. A chatham house report. November 2010 [Online]. Available at: https://www.chathamhouse.org/sites/files/chathamhouse/public/Research/International%20Security/r1110_cyberwarfare.pdf
6. Bambauer D (2011) Conundrum. Minn Law Rev 96:584. [Online]. Available at SSRN: http://ssrn.com/abstract=1807076
7. Tiirmaa-Klaar H (2013) Botnets, cybercrime and national security. In: Tiirmaa-Klaar et al. (2013) Botnets. SpringerBriefs in Cybersecurity Vol VIII, 2013
8. Watney M (2012) The way forward in addressing cybercrime regulation on a global level. J Int Technol Secured Trans (JITST) 1(1/2)
9. UNODC (2013) Comprehensive study on cybercrime. Draft—February 2013. UNODC Vienna
10. Brenner S (2007) At light speed: attribution and response to cybercrime/terrorism/warfare. J Crim L Criminol 97:379. [Online]. Available at SSRN: http://ssrn.com/abstract=1008542
11. Bendiek A (2012) European cyber security policy. SWP research paper, Stiftung Wissenschaft und Politik German Institute for international and security affairs, RP 13 October 2012 Berlin
12. Bradley T (2012) When is a cybercrime an act of cyberwar? PC World [Online]. Available at: http://www.pcworld.com/article/250308/when_is_a_cybercrime_an_act_of_cyberwar_.html
13. Maurer T (2011) Cyber norm emergence at the United Nations—An analysis of the activities at the UN regarding Cyber-security. [Online]. Available at: http://belfercenter.ksg.harvard.edu/files/maurer-cyber-norm-dp-2011-11-final.pdf
14. Jang YJ, Lim BY (2013) Harmonization among national cyber security and cybercrime response organizations: new challenges of cybercrime [Online]. Available at: Cornell University Library http://arxiv.org/abs/1308.2362
15. Office of the National Counterintelligence Executive (2011) Foreign spies stealing U.S. economic secrets in cyberspace: report to congress on foreign economic collection and industrial espionage, 2009–2011
16. Klimburg A (ed) (2012) National cyber security framework manual, NATO CCD COE Publication, Tallinn
17. e Silva K (2013) Europe's fragmented approach towards cyber security. Int Policy Rev 2(4)
18. Center for Democracy and Technology (2013) Unpacking "cybersecurity": threats, responses, and human rights considerations, 26 June 2013 [Online]. Available at: https://cdt.org/insight/unpacking-cybersecurity-threats-responses-and-human-rights-considerations/
19. OECD (2012) Cybersecurity policy making at a turning point: analysing a new generation of national cybersecurity strategies for the internet economy. OECD Publishing
20. Brosseau E (2002) Internet regulation: does self-regulation require an institutional framework. In: DRUID summer conference on "industrial dynamics of the new and old economy—who is embracing whom?" Copenhagen/Elsinore
21. Lovet G (2009) Fighting cybercrime: technical, juridical and ethical challenges. Virus bulletin conference September 2009. [Online]. Available at: http://www.fortiguard.com/sites/default/files/VB2009FightingCybercrime-Technical,Juridical and Ethical Challenges.pdf

22. Vogel J (2007) Towards a global convention against cybercrime. World conference on penal law, Guadalajara, Mexico [Online]. Available at: http://www.penal.org/IMG/Guadalajara-Vogel.pdf
23. Marsden C, Simmons S, Cave J (2006) Options for an effective-ness of internet self- and co-regulation. Phase 1 report: Mapping existing co- and self-regulatory institutions on the internet, RAND Europe [Online]. Available at: http://ec.europa.eu/dgs/information society/evaluation/data/pdf/studies/s2006 05/phase1.pdf
24. Sahel J (2006) A new policy-making paradigm for the information society. TPRC conference, 2006 [Online]. Available at: http://web.si.umich.edu/tprc/papers/2006/635/NewParadigm InfoSociety.pdf
25. Sieber U (2008) Mastering complexity in the global cyberspace: the harmonization of computer-related criminal law. In: Collection de L'UMR de Droit Compare de Paris, Bd. 15. Paris, Societe de legislation compare, pp 127–202
26. Alderson D, Soo Hoo K (2004) The role of economic incentives in securing cyberspace. Center for International Security and Cooperation, Stanford [Online]. Available at: http://cisac.fsi.stanford.edu/publications/role_of_economic_incentives_in_securing_cyberspace_the
27. Lewis J (2005) Aux armes, citoyens: cyber security and regulation in the United States. 29 Telecomm Policy 11 (2005)
28. Cornish P (2011) The vulnerabilities of developed states to economic cyber warfare. Working paper [Online]. Available at: http://www.chathamhouse.org/sites/default/files/0611wp_cornish.pdf
29. COE (2011) Global project on cybercrime, phase 2, summary [Online]. Available at: http://www.coe.int/t/dghl/cooperation/economiccrime/cybercrime/cyoctopusinterface2011/2079%20adm%20pro%20summary%2026%20Sep%202011.pdf
30. Brown A, Snower D (eds) (2011) global economic solutions 2010/2011. In: Proposals from the global economic symposium. Kiel, Germany; Kiel Institute for the World Economy. [Online]. Available at: http://www.syngentafoundation.org/__temp/Global_Economic_Solutions_2010-11.pdf
31. OECD (2011) The role of internet intermediaries in advancing public policy objectives. OECD Publishing
32. Irion K (2013) The governance of network and information security in the European Union: The European public–private partnership for resilience (EP3R) In: Gaycken S, Krueger J, Nickolay B (eds), The secure information society, Springer, Berlin 2013, p 83–116
33. Cook D (2010) Mitigating cyber-threats through public–private partnerships: low cost governance with high-impact returns. In: Proceedings of the 1st international cyber resilience conference, Edith Cowan University, Perth, Western Australia, 23 August 2010
34. Dupont B (2013) Cybersecurity futures: how can we regulate emergent risks? Technol Innovation Manage Rev July 2013, [Online]. Available at: www.timreview.ca
35. Malmström C (2012) Public–private cooperation in the fight against cybercrime. EU cybersecurity and digital crimes forum, Brussels, 31 May 2012. [Online]. Available at: http://europa.eu/rapid/press-release_SPEECH-12-409_en.htm?locale=en
36. Gercke M, Tropina T, Lozanova Y, Sund C (2011) The role of ICT regulation in addressing offences in cyberspace. In: Trends in telecommunication reform November 2010. Enabling Tomorrow's Digital World. ITU (2011)
37. Robinson N et al (2013) Data and security breaches and cyber-security strategies in the EU and its international counterparts. European Parliament, IP/A/ITRE/NT/2013-5 September 2013, PE 507.476
38. Schmidt A (2014) Open security. Contributions of networked approaches to the challenge of democratic internet security governance. In: Radu R, Chenou J-M, Weber R (eds) The evolution of global internet governance. Springer Berlin (2014)
39. Czosseck C, Ottis R, Ziolkowski K (eds) (2012) Conceptual framework for cyber defense information sharing within trust relationships. In: 2012 4th international conference on cyber conflict. 2012 NATO CCD COE Publications

40. The World Bank Group (n.d.) Global ICT department. Cybersecurity: a new model for protecting the network. [Online]. Available at: http://siteresources.worldbank.org/EXTINFORMATIONANDCOMMUNICATIONANDTECHNOLOGIES/Resources/CyberSecurity.pdf
41. Bruce R et al (2005) TNO report. International policy framework for protecting critical information infrastructure: a discussion paper outlining key policy issues, [Online]. Available at: http://www.ists.dartmouth.edu/library/158.pdf
42. Tropina T (2014) Fighting money laundering in the age of online banking, virtual currencies and internet gambling. ERA Forum 15(1):69–84
43. Fafinski S, Dutton W, Margetts H (2010) Mapping and measuring cybercrime. OII forum discussion paper no 18. [Online]. Available at: http://www.law.leeds.ac.uk/assets/files/staff/FD18.pdf
44. Coyne C, Leeson P (2005) Who's to protect cyberspace. J Law Econ Poly 1:473
45. ACMA (2011) Optimal conditions for effective self- and co-regulatory arrangements. Occasional paper. [Online]. Available at: http://www.acma.gov.au/webwr/_assets/main/lib311886/self-_and_co-regulatory_arrangements.pdf
46. Senden L (2005) Soft law, self-regulation and co-regulation in European law: where do they meet? Electron J Comp Law 9(1)
47. Bartle, I, Vass P (2007) Self-regulation and the regulatory state: a survey of policy and practice. Publ Adm 85(4):885
48. Koops B (2010) Cybercrime legislation in the Netherlands. Electron J Comp Law 14.3 (December 2010), [Online]. Available at: http://www.ejcl.org
49. Cannataci J, Bonnici J (2002) Can self-regulation satisfy the transnational requisite of successful internet regulation? In: 17th BILETA annual conference, Free University, Amsterdam, 5–6 April 2002. [Online]. Available at: www.bileta.ac.uk/02papers/cannataci.htm
50. Clinton L (n/d) Cross cutting issue #2 how can we create public private partnerships that extend to action plans that work? (undated) Int Secur Alliance. [Online]. Available at: http://www.whitehouse.gov/cyberreview/documents/
51. Brunst P, Sieber U (2010) Cybercrime legislation in Germany. In: German national reports to the XVIII. International congress of comparative law, Mohr-Siebeck, Tubingen, pp 711–800
52. Akdeniz Y (2001) Internet content regulation. UK government and the control of internet content, computer law and security report 17(5)
53. Cisco (2010) Annual security report highlighting global security threats and trends [Online]. Available at: http://www.cisco.com/en/US/prod/collateral/vpndevc/securityannualreport2010.pdf
54. Choo R (2009) The organised cybercrime threat landscape, international serious and organised crime conference 2010, [Online]. Available at: http://www.aic.gov.au/events/aic%20upcoming%20events/2010/_/media/conferences/2010-isoc/presentations/choo.pdf
55. Choo R, Smith R, Mccusker R (2007) Future directions in technology-enabled crime: 2007–09. In Res Publ Policy Ser 78:61–80
56. Seth K (2010) Evolving strategies for the enforcement of cyberlaws. High level consultation meeting for formulation of a national policy and action plan for enforcement of cyberlaw, New Delhi on 31 January 2010. [Online]. Available at: http://www.sethassociates.com/wp-content/uploads/Evolving-Strategies-for-the-Enforcement-of-Cyberlaws.pdf
57. Gotlieb R (2011) Cybercop fights organized internet crime [Online]. Available at: http://www.miller-mccune.com/legal-affairs/cybercop-fights-organized-internet-crime-27897/
58. Le Toquin J (n.d.) Public–private partnerships against cybercrime. [Online]. Available at: www.oecd.org/dataoecd/51/24/42534994.pdf
59. Thomas R (2012) Securing cyberspace though public–private partnership. A comparative analysis of partnership models May 2012 [Online]. Available at: http://csis.org/files/publication/130819_tech_summary.pdf
60. Devos S (2011) The google-NSA alliance: developing cybersecurity policy at internet speed. Fordham Intellect Prop Media Ent Law J 21(1). Article 5

61. Rosenzweig P (2011) Cybersecurity and public goods the public/private "partnership" [Online]. Available at: http://media.hoover.org/sites/default/files/documents/Emerging Threats_Rosenzweig.pdf
62. ENISA (2011) Fighting botnets: the need for global cooperation: building on EU good practices [Online]. Available at: http://www.enisa.europa.eu/activities/res/botnets/policy-statement
63. ENISA (2011) Cooperative models for effective public private partnerships good practice guide. Publications Office of the European Union, Luxembourg
64. Den Tekk K (2012) Netherlands bundles knowledge about cyber crime [Online]. Available at: http://www.rnw.nl/english/article/netherlands-bundles-knowledge-about-cyber-crime
65. NCSC (2012) The national cyber security centre (NCSC) bundles knowledge and expertise, News 02 January 2012 [Online]. Available from World Wide Web: https://www.ncsc.nl/english/current-topics/news/the-national-cyber-security-centre-ncsc-bundles-knowledge-and-expertise.html
66. Parliament of Australia (2010) Hackers, fraudsters and botnets: tackling the problem of cyber crime the report of the inquiry into cyber crime, Canberra
67. Assaf D (2008) Models of critical information infrastructure protection. Int J Crit Infrastruct Prot 1:6–14
68. Dunn-Cavelty M, Suter M (2009) Public–private partnerships are no silver bullet: an expanded governance model for critical infrastructure protection. In Int J Crit Infrastruct Prot 2(4)
69. Clinton L (2011) A relationship on the rocks: industry-government partnership for cyber defense. J Strateg Secur 4(2):97–112
70. Center for Democracy and Technology (2011) Improving our nation's cybersecurity through the public–private partnership. A white paper. March 2011 [Online]. Available at: https://www.cdt.org/files/pdfs/20110308_cbyersec_paper.pdf
71. Information Technology Industry Council (2013) ITI position paper on the proposed "directive of the European parliament and of the council concerning measures to ensure a high common level of network and information security across the union [Online]. Available at: http://www.itic.org/public-policy/cybersecurity?media=PRINT
72. Council of the European Union (2014) Note from presidency to delegations. Proposal for a directive of the European parliament and of the council concerning measures to ensure a high common level of network and information security across the union. Preparations for the 1st informal exploratory trialogue. Brussels, 3 October 2014. Interinstitutional File: 2013/0027 (COD), 13848/14 [Online]. Available at: http://www.statewatch.org/news/2014/oct/eu-council-NIS-prep-trilogue-13848-14.pdf
73. Kuschewsky M (2014) Germany. New cybersecurity law draft proposed by interior ministry. Bloomberg BNA, World data protection report 14(9), September 2014. [Online]. Available at: http://www.cov.com/files/Publication/c0b01d1b-805d-493e-90a7-f44949b7bd99/Presentation/PublicationAttachment/99bd8387-f560-4253-8189-8abbd5c19c63/New_Cybersecurity_Law_Draft_Proposed_by_Interior_Ministry.pdf
74. Gabel D, Wieczorek M, Bogusch M (2014) Germany's draft bill on IT security. White and case technology newsflash. August 2014 [Online]. Available at: http://www.whitecase.com/articles/082014/germany-draft-bill-on-it-security/#.VKKJo6BtAMR
75. Jones Day (2013) The cybersecurity debate: voluntary versus mandatory cooperation between the private sector and the federal government. A review of attempts at cybersecurity legislation and the obama administration's administrative actions. [Online]. Available at: http://www.jonesday.com/files/Publication/49c491ff-7f05-4932-9287-2c07a131e83d/Presentation/PublicationAttachment/216181fe-3cff-4535-9232-2c603c8bf48b/Cybersecurity%20Debate.pdf
76. Arthur C (2014) EU network and information security directive: is it possible to legislate for cyber security? Group briefing, October 2014. [Online]. Available at: http://www.arthurcox.com/wp-content/uploads/2014/10/Arthur-Cox-EU-Network-and-Information-Security-Directive-October-2014.pdf
77. EuroWire (2014) EU cyber security policy in the age of Snowden [Online]. Available at: http://www.bfna.org/sites/default/files/publications/EuroWire%20Jan%202014.pdf

78. Ahlert C, Marsden C, Yung C (n.d.). How 'liberty' disappeared from cyberspace: the mystery shopper tests internet content selfregulation, [Online]. Available at: http://pcmlp.socleg.ox.ac.uk/sites/pcmlp.socleg.ox.ac.uk/files/liberty.pdf

79. Doelker A (2010) Self-regulation and co-regulation: prospects and boundaries in an online environment [Online]. Available at: http://circle.ubc.ca/handle/2429/27918

80. Buckland B, Schreier F, Winkler T (2010) DCAF HORIZON 2015 working paper no. 1. [Online]. Available at: http://dspace.africaportal.org/jspui/bitstream/123456789/29509/1/Democratic%20Governance%20Challenges%20of%20Cyber%20Security.pdf?1

81. Bigo D et al (2013) National programmes for mass surveillance of personal data in EU MS and their compatibility with EU law. Study Eur Parliament 2013

82. Shore M, Du Y, Zeadally S (2011) A public–private partnership model for national cybersecurity. Policy Int J 3(2):1

83. Lukasik SJ (2011) Protecting users from the cyber commons. Commun ACM 54(9):54–61

84. Van Eeten et al (2010) The role of internet service providers in botnet mitigation an empirical analysis based on spam data. [Online]. Available at: http://www.oecd.org/LongAbstract/0,3425,en_2649_33703_46396507_119684_1_1_1,00.html

85. UNICRI (2010) Handbook to assist the establishment of public–private partnerships to protect vulnerable targets. UNICRI Publisher

Chapter 2
Evolution, Implementation and Practice of Internet Self-regulation, Co-regulation and Public–Private Collaboration

Cormac Callanan

Abstract This chapter examines the practical evolution of Internet self- and co-regulation and reflects on the current approaches in the fields of cybercrime, cybersecurity and national security. First, it provides insights into the development of self- and co-regulatory approaches to cybercrime and cybersecurity in the multi-stakeholder environment from the beginning of the Internet service provider industry. Second, it highlights the differences concerning the ecosystem of stakeholders involved in each area. Detailed analysis focuses on existing forms of collaboration, highlighting the differences and difficulties in leveraging the forms of cooperation and successful approaches from one area to another. The last part analyses the problems of multi-stakeholder approaches. It will also examine the drawbacks of the existing forms of public–private collaboration, which can be attributed to a specific area (cybercrime, cybersecurity and national security). Ultimately, this chapter provides some suggestions with regard to the way forward in self- and co-regulation in securing cyberspace. It offers unique insights into the role of Internet industry in combatting cybercrime, improving cybersecurity and supporting national security. It identifies the current practical and economic limits on cooperation between industry and state agencies and describes the balance between human rights/data privacy and crime investigation. It concludes with the challenge of state over-reaching their mandate—when national security becomes political interference in human rights.

Keywords Self-regulation · Co-regulation · Public–Private-Partnerships · Internet-Industry · Illegal Internet Content · Harmful Internet Content

© The Author(s) 2015

T. Tropina and C. Callanan, *Self- and Co-regulation in Cybercrime, Cybersecurity and National Security*, SpringerBriefs in Cybersecurity, DOI 10.1007/978-3-319-16447-2_2

2.1 The Birth of Self-regulation

2.1.1 Introduction

After 15 years of operation, there are still huge misconceptions and confusion surrounding the areas of self-regulation and co-regulation in the Internet industry. This confusion is shared among experts in the field and frequently complex debate can collapse into total disarray when it is discovered that those present have very different meanings and expectations on the area of self-regulation. Chapter 1 extensively describes the evolution and changing nature of the legislative, regulatory approaches to cybersecurity and cybercrime and the role of public–private partnerships. Whereas there are many research documents describing the different strategies to these partnerships, they sometimes seem to suggest that there was a clear long-term strategy being followed by the government and by industry representatives. However, whereas there were short-term tactics adopted relating to specific issues, much of the progress on improving cybersecurity and combating cybercrime was achieved from the constructive tensions which existed between government and industry at the beginning and then later between the variety of stakeholders actively engaged in cybersecurity and cybercrime issues. Chapter 1 rightly notes that governments were under pressure to "do something" (Sect. 1.5.2 p. 34) and this was a fundamental aspect of the early days of public–private partnerships. There was pressure to "do something" and the challenge was to determine what was that "something", who would "do" it and would it be enough to address rapidly evolving Internet challenges.

It seems appropriate therefore to start this review of self-regulation and co-regulation by looking at the definitions, consider the reason behind the persistent confusions and attempt to clarify the historical trends that have evolved to current self-regulation approaches. It started because of the government policy to support and encourage information society services and not create a chilling effect on Internet services by introducing heavy-handed regulatory issues. The main differences between styles of self-regulation are based on the stakeholders involved. It can be divided into five categories that include individual, company, industry sector, guided by regulation (sometimes called co-regulation) and multi-stakeholder.

2.1.2 Individual

Companies are led by individuals who decide on their own interpretation of what would be appropriate policy or ethics for their organisation. They choose this based on the assessment of the consumer base and the changing needs of the company over time. The strength of this approach is that there is strong commitment to self-regulation but the weakness is that it varies over time, does not have a consistent approach over time and changes as senior managers change.

2.1.3   Company

Self-regulation is performed at a company level where decisions are made by the company management board which decides what elements of self-regulation are appropriate for their organisation based on the company ethics profile and understanding of corporate social responsibility (CSR). The strength of this approach is that there is strong commitment and greater consistency over time. In addition, the organisation knows more about the specific area of technology and how it can be abused and the possibilities for positive action. The weakness is that it is directly related to current market conditions and is more relevant for large multinationals than small (less than 100 employees) organisations. This system has the challenge that there is no consistent approach for all organisations which can be monitored and measured for effectiveness. The policies are not always published and they can vary significantly between countries of operation. Another weakness of this approach is that it can turn important societal issues into competitive market positioning activities.

2.1.4   Industry Sector

Self-regulation is determined by a coordinated industry approach. Individual organisations come together to discuss and agree a common approach to specific issues. Once agreed, these areas of common interest can be implemented by a shared organisation with a mandate to implement the agreed protocols or to represent the group of organisations in an agreed manner. There can be agreed membership procedures, funding structures and regular meetings to share knowledge and concerns and agree policies. There can be common codes of conduct and ethics, and there can be complaint procedures against the activities or behaviours of one of the members of that shared organisation. The strength of this approach is the common consistent approach by a range of industry players, which is a powerful response to agreed issues. The weakness is that it takes longer to agree a common profile on certain issues. There can be issues that have different levels of impact to different members and therefore have different levels of urgency. There is also a concern that the industry body is only interested in the best interests of the industry and not in the broader needs of the society which can lead to concerns about transparency and accountability. In addition, many countries prevent corporations to act in collusion in the marketplace and therefore, the areas of common interest need to be very narrowly focused and clearly focused on areas of societal interest and not on business behaviours or the potential unintentional creation of a cartel.

2.1.5 Guided by Regulation (Sometimes Called Co-regulation)

This approach brings together the role of government and the role of the industry sector whereby there is a role for government stakeholders to participate in the discussions to form policy for the industry sector. This can be further enhanced by the implementation of legislation on which the fundamentals of industry responsibility are detailed with motivations and sanctions clearly outlined. Often these regulations or legislative initiatives are first discussed with the industry and designed to have reasonable and fair impact on all industry members with a clear responsibility for action and liability for non-compliance. The strength of this approach is that there is a consistent approach to (self-) regulation over time and that the industry has external oversight to ensure progress on issues causing major inter-organisation disagreement. In addition, there is a wider range of expertise available to state organisations sharing their collective knowledge and experiences to develop the best possible response. A major weakness is that it is difficult to respond to issues in a timely manner and that there might not be an adequate range of competencies in the industry or state stakeholders.

2.1.6 Multi-stakeholder

This multi-stakeholder grouping takes the strengths of the previous groupings and expands the stakeholders to include experts from a range of other areas of society. This brings a broader range of expertise to the discussions and responds to issues about transparency, accountability and oversight of industry behaviour. However, the downside of this approach is that there is a larger, diverse grouping of experts which can take longer to be fully apprised of the range of aspects of an individual problem, and there is an even wider range of political, social and personal interests that is brought into discussion. In addition, those affected (both financially and legally) by the final decisions are often the minority voice in the debate.

It can be seen that there a wide range of approaches to self-regulation and co-regulation which offer different levels of transparency, accountability, oversight and effectiveness. These different approaches evolved over time and continue to be in use today. Many of these approaches are used in parallel and can be very confusing to the observer. To understand how these approaches worked in practice, the evolution of Internet services needs to be considered.

2.1.7 Background

In 1996, I had just completed the sale of my Internet company called IEunet (EUnet Ireland) in Dublin, Ireland. My business partner and I had started the first commercial Internet business in Ireland, recognising the importance of the Internet to business, in 1991. Business was hectic with Internet access provided over analogue modems for services such as Gopher, email and FTP. The arrival of the web protocols in 1991 had a dramatic effect on traffic profiles. We started the company with modems operating at 1200 baud, and by the time we sold the company in 1996, the modems were operating at 57,600 baud and the international bandwidth was very expensive. ISDN services were also becoming popular. Broadband to the home was still a distant dream. Self-regulation in those days was unheard of and mostly it was based on internal company reactions to changing customer requirements in problems identified in the network. So the first understanding of self-regulation was that a single company would endeavour to ensure that their view of acceptable moral and legal standards was enforced against customers of their service.

Already the arrival of home user consumers onto the Internet was causing significant impact. The user profile for these users was quite significantly different. Business users had a clear business focus and interest in a reliable service as the primary interest. They accessed the Internet during the day using computers controlled by their business, and the contact between our network and theirs was often performed between technically competent personnel in their IT department and our network operations centre engineers. During this phase, telecom companies were not paying attention to the Internet since they could neither understand the business model of the Internet nor the use of the technologies such as freeware and shareware neither purchased nor supported by tier-1 software and hardware multinationals. Traditional telecom companies focused their service sales in the data carrier area on X25 and X400 with clear, expensive charging models. Equipment to implement X25 and X400 was expensive and data were priced on packets sent and received (international sharing). However, it was very true to say that a telecom company depended on the flexibility and reliability of their billing systems to be successful. Such systems tracked resource usage and, more importantly, ensured that all such usage was charged to the correct customer.

The arrival of the HTTP protocol (the web) and the first mass-market versions of NCSA Mosaic in January 1993 had a dramatic effect on the Internet businesses and changed the Internet forever.

My company had a small and growing turnover with a loyal customer base accessing a range of core services. Around 1992, there was increasing demand for online connectivity to Internet services with increasing requests and sales of dedicated leased lines from customers to connect to the Internet and to be online 24/7, enabling the provision of business web services by our customer base. Facing into substantial investment to maintain sufficient international bandwidth at a time when telecom companies across Europe were still state-owned monopolies, and increase staffing to support the growth, we had the opportunity to sell our business to a company who later sold the business on to a telecom company in the next years. The arrival of online services and phenomenal interest in the Internet attracted the attention and interest of traditional telecom operators.

2.1.8 Content versus Traffic

Before 1993, the primary services on the Internet were mainly text focused and included email, Usenet News and Gopher. Graphic image files could be exchanged between users by breaking them into equal chunks of data like pieces of a jigsaw puzzle transmitting them in different news or email messages and then re-combining the pieces back together to recreate the original image. There was dedicated software that would dissect and reconstitute a range of files to/from an individual document.

2.1.9 Usenet News

Usenet News was where active publicly visible self-regulation began with technical blocking and content assessment. This is explained in more detail in the next chapter but is introduced here. Usenet News had very high volumes of traffic consuming as much as 40 % of international bandwidth and storage capacity on the core network systems. It took up a significant amount of operations engineers' time to support and maintain the smooth flowing information content and the increasingly large number of news topic. Each customer could select which newsgroups to include in their news feeds and also which ones could be blocked and not updated. In the beginning, newsgroups focused on sharing technical tips and tricks between computing specialists and sharing free software tools (using chopping-into-chunks and reconstruction). However, over time, due to its success in the technical area, newsgroups were created for hobbies and crafts (fishing, chess, gaming, knitting and cooking) and for discussion and debate on a wide range of social issues (poverty, global warming, air travel, politics and sex).

Newsgroup traffic volumes across international lines and local disk storage were constantly monitored. The quality and capacity of an ISP and the number of days of newsgroup storage were among the key performance criteria when selecting an Internet service provider. A flurry of activity and vibrant interchange of ideas on newsgroups over a weekend or holiday could easily consume over 90 % of international bandwidth or over 90 % of available expensive disk space, thereby blocking other activities on the systems. In the beginning, users would usually decide to take all newsgroups and, then over time, in order to reduce bandwidth consumption and storage requirement, they would reduce the number of days stored and updated and then reduce the range of newsgroups over time. Several newsgroups including newsgroups related to software development (alt.binaries, alt.binaries.images, music, etc.,) generated large volumes of large messages since some documents/programs could be broken into over 50 individual message chunks. As a result, it was easier over time to determine which specific newsgroups consumed the most resources. This is my earliest memory of the beginning of the online sex/pornography debate.

The newsgroup hierarchy[1] had many groups dedicated to sex-related content including but not limited to pornographic material. Initially, it covered discussions about sex with separate discussions about homosexuality or celibacy or pregnancy or sexual health. Some of these newsgroups were moderated but the majority of the newsgroups were not. The issues of homosexuality or abortion were topics of passionate debate in Ireland during those days and our company was apprehensive about the legal standing and potential liability of hosting newsgroup discussions on these topics. It is not a surprise therefore that sexual content and the issue of legality were considered as intrinsic to Internet self-regulation evolution. It is not true to say that these issues were constantly debated inside the company, but the issue of the legal uncertainty around some type of sex-related content was occasionally debated over coffee. I have no recollection of any legally qualified professionals at that time having sufficient knowledge or understanding of Internet technologies in order to be able to form coherent comprehensive legal advice based on the state of the Irish legal system. It was not realistic for the company to have a clear legal understanding of what was or what was not legal on online services.

By 1992, there were over 15,000 different newsgroup titles divided into different news hierarchies, and bandwidth consumption became a serious concern for the Internet backbone systems. It was decided that the company needed to conserve bandwidth by reducing the number of newsgroups being carried and therefore accessible to consumers. This then created a debate about which specific newsgroups would be "dropped" (the word "blocked" had not been invented yet!). This started the debate on two other issues which became major issues for the future. These are consumer profiling and freedom of speech. My Internet business sold services primarily to companies, but a small number of customers were individuals who had adopted the Internet early.

There were two ways to access news—one way was to take a news feed and select/identify which newsgroup hierarchies or even specific newsgroups to subscribe to. The contents of these newsgroups were then transferred to the customer's system for later reading or expiration. There were no records available on our system about which individual news items were read or archived by the customer.

---

[1]Additional technical details is available on http://en.wikipedia.org/wiki/Usenet (last accessed 11 Dec 2014).

2.1.10 Log Records and Charging

In the second access method, a customer would access the hierarchy stored in our systems using newsgroup client software. These systems would leave log records to identify which newsgroup had been accessed and which specific news items were read by each consumer. Broadly speaking, no one was deliberately analysing these logs to monitor individual organisations or people. The log files were designed to determine errors with the communications. Many log files were very vague or inaccurate and were used to diagnose specific technical performance issue. However, our ISP charged users a flat rate for a news feed and separately charged in volume groups for email transmission and receipt. We therefore used the log records to determine the volume and quantity of emails sent and received per customer. In fact, we became so good at this that we generated monthly summary usage reports for our customers which were sent with their monthly invoice! We would then plan future invoicing structures with our customers based on these usage reports generated by detailed log analysis. At this phase of evolution, therefore, we became aware of the level of business information and personally or business-sensitive information, which was being recorded by the core network systems, and the need for security, privacy, confidentiality and data protection acumen across the organisation. We instilled in all staff the need for respect for privacy in a similar way as a bank would train new staff. The concern at this time was to build trust and confidence with users and businesses to encourage adaption of Internet services. It was by no means certain that Internet services would survive and evolve.

Many of the Internet structures—DNS, ip-allocation, international routing agreements—were still based on academia and managed by highly competent, motivated individuals on a voluntary basis. It was not obvious which Internet services could be productised and priced at acceptable levels both for the consumer and the business selling the service to be adequately profitable. In fact, the concept of selling access to the Internet was frowned on by many of the grandfathers of the Internet who were aghast on the issue of allowing commercial entities to pollute the purity of online research depending on the Internet, or shocked at the concept of selling Internet like it was a product or a commodity—almost like prostitution!

2.1.11 Traditional Telecom Services

On the other side of the debate, the national telecommunications operators operated in a monopolist environment. Usually a national telecommunications company was owned, operated and directly controlled by the state and was licenced, regulated and authorised to exclusively sell telecommunications services to the general public. Phone lines were not readily available across the Irish state and often incurred delays of over 6 months to get a phone line installed. All telecom workers were state employees and were required to sign the official secrets act when they started their career in telecommunications. These telecom operators sold several core services including voice and data on a monopoly basis.

Many of these telecommunications services had different levels of volume purchasing from a single voice channel/line at the low end and over 30–100 voice channels at the high end. In the data area, one could use an X25 circuit across a dedicated phone line or the cash-rich organisations could purchase dedicated leased lines from telecom to connect your business to your customer or perhaps your headquarters. Dial-up modem connections or dedicated leased lines from telecom were the only ways that users could connect to the Internet. We offered Internet services and our connection to the global Internet was through a leased line to the UK and later a dedicated leased line to the central EUnet network operations centre in Amsterdam, thereby linking us to other countries connected into Amsterdam across Europe. EUnet then operated a fixed line to the USA. The cost of an international telecommunications link was exorbitant. We worked to ensure the maximum efficiency and usage of these links and they were the major expenditure of our business. If one includes the rental costs of dial-up phone lines (which reached 30 lines at one point) and the other lines installed on behalf of customers, the overall expenditure on telecommunication by my company was enormous. We were also totally dependent on those links for business connectivity and when links failed, we strived to maintain a professional, courteous relationship with Telecom Eireann who supplied and maintained these services for us. By the mid-1990s, it became clear to telecommunications companies that X25/X400 services were faltering and failing to achieve significant market penetration or acceptance. It also became clear, with the phenomenal growth of the web technologies released to the world in 1992, that the Internet usage was increasing exponentially across the world and challenging and undermining established Telecom product sales and services. This became a problem when telecommunications operators were forced to accept that they needed to embrace the Internet and then begin offering a basic range of Internet services to their client base. Although there was a range of in-house skills available to offer basic communications services such as modems, ISDN and dedicated leased circuits, there was less skill available to manage the TCP IP protocols or the higher level applications such as news, email and web.

Telecommunications companies had a long history of working closely with state agencies and implementing government policy since they were owned and regulated by the government. Employees were considered as state employees. This relationship became very influential in the growth of self-regulation initiatives across Europe. However, telecommunications companies were more comfortable with a clear government-mandated regulatory environment with which they had a lot of experience and familiarity. On the other hand, the new Internet companies had little experience of self-regulation, had suffered first-hand effects of a monopolistic telecommunications market and expected that a regulatory-driven environment would be biased towards telecommunications companies and against creative, evolving information society services coming from the Internet. This tension became an essential element of the evolution of self-regulation.

2.1.12 Open Telecommunications Market

Although the national incumbent telecom provider still had a monopoly to offer network connections and home voice telecom services, the laws and regulations in the area of data services were not so clear. Organisations could access international leased lines by leasing a line locally to a distribution point and gain access to international bandwidth through that point. These would use the services of a growing range of international carriers—often the national carriers in other European countries competing with each other on international services. Once a dedicated leased line was purchased by a company in Ireland, there were few restrictions of what services or communications protocols could be implemented on that line. For example, one service provided by my company was Internet services and others included offering pay as you use international voice services. This bypassed local regulation by first requiring a customer to dial a local number, enter a pin code and then input the desired international number. These type of services undercut the profit margins of the national telecom company and drew direct attention to the major technological upheavals being experienced by the telecom sector across Europe. In summary, although telecom was a monopoly in each country across Europe, there was a wide range of technological options available to encourage increased competition between national carriers competing international and other embryonic operations at a national level. As the market became more open, there was increasing business competition in what became known as "other licenced operations—OLOs", which is still in use today.

2.1.13 Dropping Newsgroups

During 1993, our international bandwidth was insufficient for the volume of traffic, incurred heavy usage on a 24 × 7 basis. Since we focused on business clients, we managed the traffic to offer highest possible quality of service to the customers during office hours and reassigned system requirements to out-of-office-hours slots. This included system backups, system upgrades and even newsgroup transfers to/ from our international providers. This traffic shaping was a crude human-managed manual activity that strived to achieve the most efficient usage of available resources—bandwidth and storage. This initiative drew our focus towards the newsgroup system and regular technical monitoring and reporting. We monitored fluctuations on newsgroup message volumes and fluctuations on message size. We noted the growing number of newsgroups titles and the increase in newsgroups of a social nature or dealing with recreations such as football, volleyball, basketball, fishing, cycling and swimming. The newsgroup system was a subject of every management meeting, and most discussions were about ways to minimise its effect on our scarce and valuable system resources. The company continued the traffic shaping policy by providing different level of services between different sections of the newsgroup hierarchies—to improve the overall impact on the quality of services. We decided that we would only update some high-volume hierarchies during night-time hours but ensure some hierarchies in regular use by our customers continued to be updated during less busy traffic times throughout the day. Most of the customers accepted and understood this change as an overall service improvement. Since our service targeted business customers, the primary target areas for newsgroup efficiencies were focused on those non-business, socially focused newsgroups. A clean differentiation was not always possible, and we sometimes received requests for specific newsgroups to be updated more frequently which we accommodated.

However, newsgroup volumes continued to grow, and we eventually decided to drop some newsgroups completely from our service. The first newsgroups we dropped were those groups with very large volume of very large size messages causing a noticeable spike in using system resources. A cursory examination of the title/name of these newsgroups indicated that the material related to explicit sexual content including both images and text. This type of content incurred phenomenal growth on the Internet, and this was a wide range from soft-porn images to what is known as hard-porn and even what later became known as illegal content. We stopped carrying these newsgroups. Publicly, the explanation for this decision was the significant impact on scarce system resources caused by the volume of content in these newsgroups. In addition, since the business sector was our primary target market there was no interest by these customers in these newsgroups. Privately, we lived in a country where printed pornography was banned, homosexuality was a criminal offence and contraception was strictly regulated. Our business was licenced but arguably in a very unclear legal area of telecommunication services potentially restricted by the state. We were concerned that the additional complexity of hosting content (for a business service of little business benefit) might draw undesirable attention from various state agencies. Therefore, when we made our public announcement among many other technical updates, we wondered whether we would receive any complaints from our customer base or even debate of the newsgroups we selected to be no longer carried on our service. There were no major concerns expressed from any of the customers although it was noted by many that the range of newsgroups being carried had changed. Many customers had already noted the increasing volumes and the subsequent impact on their own resources and saw the changed list as an opportunity to regularise their own systems and reached a similar conclusion to the content choice.

2.1.14   Embryonic Self-regulation

At this time, around 1993–1994, we had faced the difficult choice of basic, elementary self-regulation and faced up to specific decisions relating to content. These two issues were the major challenge found by the Internet service providers across Europe. Most of the owners and managers were not adequately trained or skilled in debating the challenging nuances between freedom of speech and human rights or not carrying certain type of content—where a choice was possible. Most of the Internet service providers believed that the service they provided was defined according to their own choice. They did not accept or acknowledge that they had a public duty to carry content without personal bias to different types of content. In these early years, they knew nothing of the debates around the net-neutrality and managed those Internet services as their own little dominion. There were some balancing aspects. Traditional telecom operators were not held liable for content or behaviours exercised using their technical infrastructure. For example, bomb threats, suicide or harassment phone calls were not considered an issue of liability for the telecommunications operator but of the person who committed the act. As long as the operator played no active role in causing those phone calls to occur, it was considered that they were exempt from liability. This was known as common carrier status. Many Internet service providers assumed that they would be considered as common carriers by operators, regulatory authorities, governments and in the Courts if there was any legal challenge. There was a corollary to this issue of common carrier status, which became a major issue in later debates on self-regulation. Whereas an ISP would not be held liable for content carried on their networks which they had not initiated or directly requested, they might introduce liability for themselves if they voluntarily chose to take steps to manage or control the large volumes of diverse content and activities that take place on their networks. In other words, if you take and accept any responsibility for content—no matter how minor—the protection afforded by the common carrier status might be considered as waived.

Much of all these legal musings and ramblings were not based on specific facts or legal texts or a deep academic understanding of international human rights law or commercial contracts. It was based on hearsay, collected wisdoms and shared discussions among staff in the international EUnet networks and issues which arose for different network members during these early developmental years of Internet services. I remember being asked by EUnet to take responsibility to specify and define the exact descriptions of the services which we were selling to customers across Europe in order for us to learn more about the possible options, charging models, revenue models and actual cost for each service and variation in each service. This was a mammoth task which succeeded in highlighting the large variety of services and the complex range of options on offer across Europe. It is reasonable and fair to note that most of the members of EUnet were more focused on business growth and overcoming daily technical challenges than philosophical debates relating to content. Although it was increasingly clear that Internet services were experiencing exponential demand, it was not clear if there was a financial/revenue sustaining model, which would work for the individual member of the EUnet network. Although there were occasional debates about content issues, these focused almost exclusively on the impacts relating to service efficiency and on the financial bottom line rather than the nature of the content itself. Other members of the EUnet network did not have any technical, or system or network resources in carrying a full newsgroup feed and did not have to make a choice over which newsgroups to drop and which to carry. So they continued to carry and distribute a full newsgroup feed until newsgroups became the first open battle in the area of self-regulation. This occurred in the UK and is described in detail in the next section. In Ireland, the newsgroup service continued with the reduced selection of newsgroups. When we later purchased extra bandwidth, the newsgroup list was restored to a full service for a short period of time, but as the additional bandwidth also came under pressure from traffic volumes, the news feed was reduced again.

2.1.15 Anecdote

Almost a year after this policy was initiated, I received a request for a meeting with one customer relating to newsgroups. I remember being very curious how the meeting would unfold. I incorrectly assumed that we would discuss the selection process we had used and whether there were any hidden biases or phobias in favour of or against one religious morality or social ethos which was a constant issue of public discourse throughout the 1980s and 1990s in Ireland. The person I met was a young man dressed like a student. He was quiet spoken and slightly nervous. The theme of the meeting was the newsgroup policy. To my surprise, he understood that we had blocked some groups which seemed to accept/support/encourage child sex abuse; he also noted that other content relating to adult content, homosexuality, etc. was morally difficult to determine. He explained that he had come to request me to restore one newsgroup to the unblocked lists. Whereas he accessed this newsgroup on our service before, he could still access the newsgroup through international news services. He explained to me that the group he was referring to might appear similar to the other newsgroups in that area. However, it focused on supporting victims of child sexual abuse and coping and recovery strategies. I was told that he had been abused when he was younger and was now dealing with the impact and effects on his life, and this newsgroup helped him share with others and learn from others who had suffered similar pains to him. After he left my office, I was quite taken by his story and I remember reflecting on the complexity of online content issues and the complexity of assuming the mantel of guardian of moral rights without oversight, transparency and accountability. It was clear to me that the issue of content was a major challenge for the Internet. It was also clear that the challenges were diverse and divisive with many conflicting debates with few clear obvious solutions. All these early minor forays into issues surrounding content and self-regulation were the beginning of a large time of my life spent debating and encouraging practical solutions for *illegal and harmful content* and activity on the Internet.

2.1.16 Conclusion

In the early 1990s, the benefits of Internet access for business were clear. Email began to replace facsimile (fax) and there was incredible growth in free software tools available on the Internet. Microsoft had initially denied that TCP/IP protocol had any relevance to their business, later recanted and released TCP/IP support in the NT 3.1 release. Users on Windows 3.x and Windows Millennium needed to install extra software to use TCP/IP and dial-up services to use the Internet. In spite of the obstacles facing users of mainstream operating systems, the Internet was enthusiastically adopted and grew out of academia spread into business services and had finally been taken into the home. The price of personal computers was high, modems were expensive and reasonably priced Internet software was difficult to find and configure. The first home users were users who had access at work and were instantly convinced of the importance of Internet access to communicate with colleges around the world, and by using Usenet News and Gopher could stay up to date with the latest hardware and software developments. My company did not target home users, but we had several customers who paid expensive subscription to access the Internet from home. Some of these had the subscription paid by their companies. However, a company was started in 1993 called Ireland Online with a specific mandate to target home customers and small businesses. In the first years of their existence, they purchased their upstream connection from my company, but in the later years they purchased their own international bandwidth to the UK.

By the mid-1990s, the price of modems had dramatically dropped with the lower priced US Robotics modem at 21 Kbps speed in 1992. This speed increased to 38.8 Kbps and later 56 Kbps modems around the same time as 64 K ISDN lines from Telecom Eireann became available. However, the cost of international bandwidth had only reduced marginally since the telecommunications market was still a monopoly environment. The evolution of the Internet had reached a point where modems were now affordable, the software and hardware needed to access the Internet were more accessible and were also understandable by the ordinary user, and the HTTP web protocol was released to the world enabling easier dissemination of multimedia content on the Internet than ever before. With this wonderful availability of options, the drive towards Internet adoption accelerated and Internet growth patterns started to grow exponentially. It became an amazing stressful roller-coaster time of business growth, user expectations and demands and endless frustrations with slow networks, failing modem connections, long downloads and bandwidth utilisation charts which seemed to flatline at 100 % usage. My enduring memory of those times was the stress and the endless pent-up demand and the amazing new ideas that unfolded each day at work. It was an amazing time of technological creativity.

In 1996, the company was sold to a market investor and I stood down as owner and manager. The company had grown over 5 years to one of Ireland's leading Internet service companies. The societal challenges caused by content on the Internet were clear to see. There were daily technology improvements and Internet adoption figures continued to grow exponentially. The Internet was here to stay and brought a range of new challenges to the society. Society was not prepared for many of these.

2.2   Self-regulation Matures

2.2.1   Introduction

From 1996 onwards, self-regulation activities became more focused and were publicly debated with extensive engagement by intergovernmental organisations (Council of Europe, European Union, OSCE, United Nations, etc.), national governments and law enforcement. The subject of these discussions is related to the role of the Internet industry and the need for concrete practical action against concerns relating to the Internet. Unfortunately, there was a dearth of actual clear societal and governmental policies or a clear identifiable target of specific concern. The growing awareness of the volume of child pornography on the Internet became a focus of this concern and the common shared focus and interest of desirable direct action and effective response. Child abuse was not a new crime since it had previously happened in closed secretive environments, and before the arrival of images of child abuse (child pornography), the only way it was discovered and investigated was when sufficient trust was placed in the word of the abused child. The widespread creation and distribution of child pornography—the images of a crime scene—on the Internet had an enormously shocking impact on people around the world, and many Internet service providers chose to take steps to combat such content and activity.

2.2.2   Putting Structure on Self-regulation

On **24 April 1996**, at the informal European Council meeting held in Bologna, the European Telecommunications and Culture ministers identified the issue of illegal and harmful content on the Internet as an urgent priority. The European Council then requested the European Commission "to produce a summary of problems posed by the rapid development of the Internet and to assess, in particular, the desirability of Community or international regulation".

2.2.3   UK French Letter

On **9 August 1996**, the Metropolitan Police Service in the UK sent out a famous letter[2] which became known as the "French letter" to all Internet service providers about pornographic material on the Internet specifically relating to newsgroup content and requesting that 133 newsgroups[3] would no longer be distributed.

---

[2]http://textfiles.com/magazines/CUD/cud0862.txt.

[3]http://www.computerworld.co.nz/article/519610/british_police_list_133_obscene_newsgroups/ (last accessed 8 Dec 2014).

The letter shown in the box was a defining moment in the history of self-regulation. In essence, the Metropolitan Police Service had identified a list of 133 newsgroups which they believed were pornographic in nature and would likely be illegal under the obscene publications act in the UK. They acknowledge that the content in the newsgroup was continually changing and then requested the Internet service providers to monitor these newsgroups in order to "take necessary action against those others found to contain such material". According to Richard Barry in the Independent[4] on 2 September 1996, "the police argue that under the Obscene Publications Act and the Protection of Children Act, the ISPs are breaking the law and must act to stop the material from being accessed".

This was a very interesting development in the history of self-regulation for Internet service providers located in the United Kingdom and across Europe since this was the first time that it had been suggested that they would be held liable for content they host or content they carry on their services. It was not clear how broad this liability would stretch, and at the time, there was significant concern that such liability would have a huge chilling effect on Internet growth and Internet adoption by users. It is worth noting that the letter referred to a broad range of pornographic content which was not limited or bounded in any way. There are a number of intriguing issues relating to this initiative:

- A national police force had taken upon itself the right and responsibility to request an Internet service provider not to distribute the contents of a list of newsgroups identified by the police and specified by name. It did not appear that this was implemented as a result of a specific government policy or mandate, but was an effort to enforce the rule that what was illegal offline was also illegal online.
- This introduced the role of police to proactively prevent potential online criminal activity with no direct engagement with the judiciary processes.
- It introduced the concept of notice and takedown relating to illegal content.
- Liability for the Internet service providers was linked to the concept of actual knowledge of illegal online activities.
- It was further stated that the list might change depending on the changing nature of the content of such groups and that the police expect ISPs to continuously monitor newsgroups and to remove those which contain illegal materials. This was a major concern since it suggested that the Internet service providers should proactively monitor their networks for illegal activity and raised the spectre of widespread pervasive monitoring with its obvious conflict with human rights.
- That an ISP would be considered the publisher of such material and therefore likely to be liable for publication of such content.
- It was implicitly suggested by the police that this was their understanding of what they considered to be self-regulation by the industry players.
- There was clear threat of enforcement if the request was ignored.

---

[4]http://www.independent.co.uk/life-style/the-list-and-the-hysteria-1361446.html (last accessed 8 Dec 2014).

```
Date--    9th August 1996

METROPOLITAN POLICE SERVICE

Clubs and Vice Unit
Charing Cross Police Station
Agar Street
London WC2N 4JP

Telephone: 0171 321 7752
Facsimile:  0171 321 7762

To: All Internet Service Providers


Dear Sir / Madam

Pornographic Material on the Internet

Further to the seminar held at New Scotland Yard on 2nd August I
enclose, as promised by Superintendent Mike Hoskins, a list of those
Newsgroups which we believe contain pornographic material.

We have attempted to confirm that the Newsgroups listed currently
contain this offensive material but as you will be only too aware the
content is continually changing and you will need to satisfy yourself
about the nature and content before taking any action. Furthermore, this
list is not exhaustive and we are looking to you to monitor your
Newsgroups identifying and taking necessary action against those others
found to contain such material. As you will be aware the publication of
obscene articles is an offence.

This list is only the starting point and we hope, with the co-operation
and assistance of the industry and your trade organisations, to be
moving quickly towards the eradication of this type of Newsgroup from
the Internet. At the seminar we debated the means of maintaining an up
to date list and you will recall that ISPA volunteered to pool
information and assist in this initiative. However, we are very anxious
that all service providers should be taking positive action now, whether
or not they are members of a trade association.
```

At this time, there were approximately 1.3 million[5] Internet subscribers in the UK. There was real concern with European ISPs that this national enforcement action might be applied to the Internet service providers across Europe. Jim Dixon from VBCnet[6] in the UK stated that *"While we do not disagree that the articles in some of these groups are often objectionable, we disagree in principle with this form of censorship"*. He urged all customers to make it clear *"why these news groups have been withdrawn and we urge you to contact your MPs and the media about this arbitrary action by the police. If there is no protest, if a precedent is established, the UK Internet is going to fall under the control of the Clubs and Vice Unit at Charing Cross Police Station"*. The list is shown in Appendix I, and a quick

---

[5]http://news.cnet.com/U.K.-banning-133-newsgroups/2100-1023_3-221558.html (last accessed 8 Dec 2014).
[6]Ibid.

review shows a list of content subjects relating to diverse sexual content and activity including illegal child abuse material. Some of the newsgroups referred to text newsgroups about homosexual activity, which was perfectly legal in the UK. It was a surprise at the time since newsgroups were diminishing in use, and usage of the World Wide Web was growing exponentially; there was real concern that causing Internet service providers liable for content on the Internet would have a major chilling effect on Internet adoption. It created a real debate in the Internet service provider industry about the possibilities for Internet blocking and Internet liability. It was known by both the Metropolitan police and the UK Internet service providers that users could still gain access to the full newsgroup list and content by accessing a newsgroup provider outside the UK based in a different European country or based outside Europe completely.

2.2.4 UK Child Pornography Laws [1][7]

- In the UK, the Sexual Offences (Conspiracy & Incitement) Act 1996 became law in June 1996. Section 2 of the Act made it an offence to incite another person to commit certain sexual acts against children outside the UK. Section 2 extended the scope of incitement to ensure that any incitement by means of a telephone call, fax, Internet message or similar method is considered to have taken place in the UK if the message was received in the UK.
- The Protection of Children Act 1978 was passed in response to the growing problem of child pornography. Its main purpose was to close some potential gaps in the measures available to police and prosecutors. The definition of "photograph" given in Section 7(4) of the 1978 Act was extended to include photographs in electronic data format following the amendments made by Section 84 (4) of the Criminal Justice and Public Order Act 1994 (CJPOA 1994).
- The CJPOA 1994 introduced the concept of "pseudo-photographs" of children. Pseudo-photographs are technically photographs, but they are created by computer software manipulating one or more pre-existing pictures. For example, a child's face can be superimposed on an adult body, or to another child's body, with the characteristics of the body altered to create pornographic computer-generated images without the involvement of a real child. It is now an offence "for a person to take, or permit to be taken or to make, any indecent photographs or pseudo-photographs of a child; (or) to distribute or show such indecent photographs or pseudo-photographs" under Section 1 of the 1978 Act.[8]

---

[7]http://www.cyber-rights.org/reports/governan.htm (last accessed 7 Dec 2014). Akdeniz [1].

[8]Idem. ("*The UK police believed that the creators or possessors of pseudo-photographs would end up abusing children, so the purpose of the new legislation may be seen as to criminalise acts preparatory to abuse, and also to close possible future loopholes in the prosecution of such cases, as it may be very difficult to separate a pseudo-photograph from a real photograph.*

- As per Section 160 of the Criminal Justice Act 1988 Under Section 160 of the 1988 Act as amended by Section 84(4) of the CJPOA 1994, it is an offence for a person to have an indecent photograph or pseudo-photograph of a child in his possession. This offence is a serious arrestable offence with a maximum imprisonment term not exceeding 6 months.

Against this background, the European Commission produced a communication looking at the challenge of harmful and illegal Internet content.

2.2.5 *The Protection of Minors and Human Dignity in Audio-Visual Services*

The informal EC council meeting held in Bologna was followed by the informal meeting of Ministers of Justice and Home Affairs **on 26 and 27 September 1996** in Dublin during the 5th Irish Presidency of the European Union (EU), from July through December 1996, which discussed further cooperation between Member States to combat trade in human beings and sexual abuse of children.

On **23 October 1996**, the Commission produced a communication on "illegal and harmful content on the Internet" and a Green Paper on "the Protection of Minors and Human Dignity in Audio-Visual and Information services". The Communication on Illegal and Harmful Content on the Internet, (Com (96) 487) in October 1996 and the Green Paper on the, Protection of Minors and Human Dignity in Audio-Visual and Information Services (Com (96) 483.) set the scene for all European initiatives in this area over the next decade from 1995 to 2005.

Two main types of preparatory work were carried out for the Green Paper. Firstly, the Member States were asked to reply to a questionnaire on the protection of minors and human dignity in the context of the development of services in the information society. All of the Member States responded favourably to this

---

(Footnote 8 continued)

Although pseudo-photographs can be created without the involvement of real children, there is a justifiable fear that harm to children is associated with all child pornography. The Williams Committee stated:

'Few people would be prepared to take the risk Querywhere children are concerned and just as the law recognised that children should be protected against sexual behaviour which they are too young to properly consent to, it is almost universally agreed that this should apply to participation in pornography.'

On the other hand, there are arguments that pseudo-photographs are not harmful. The children involved in child pornography may suffer physical or mental injury, but with pseudo-photographs, the situation is quite different. These photographs are created only by the use of computers. There is no involvement of children in production and there is no direct harm to children in their use. However there is substantial evidence that photographs of children engaged in sexual activity are used as tools for the further molestation of other children, and photographs or pseudo-photographs will be used interchangeably for this purpose.").

consultation processes. Secondly, with a view to the preparation of this Green Paper, the Commission commissioned a series of studies on the protection of minors and human dignity in the information society. These cover the regulatory, economic and technological aspects of the question in the 15 Member States, Canada, Japan and the USA. The Green Paper looked at the broader audio-visual services including radio, terrestrial and satellite television services and the Internet.

The Green Paper set out to examine the challenges that society faces in ensuring that two specific issues of overriding public interest, i.e. protection of minors and of human dignity, are adequately taken into account in the rapidly evolving world of audio-visual and information services. It was presented at the same time as the "Commission Communication on Illegal and harmful Content on Internet". The two documents were fully complementary, both as regards timing and scope. The fight against the dissemination of content offensive to human dignity and the protection of minors—against exposure to content that is harmful to their development—were considered of fundamental importance in enabling new audio-visual and information services to develop in a climate of trust and confidence. It underlined the need not to confuse problems that are different in nature, such as child pornography, which is illegal and subject to penal sanctions, and children accessing pornographic content for adults, which while being harmful for their development may not be illegal for adults. It points out that national arrangements in Europe are all set against the background of the fundamental rights enshrined in the European Convention of Human Rights (ECHR) which are incorporated in general principles of Community law by Article F.2 of the Treaty on European Union. In particular, Article 10 ECHR guarantees the right to freedom of expression. In the fight against illegal content, cooperation between the Member States in the field of justice and home affairs was identified as having a fundamental role to play given the international character of the new services. The potential for encouraging cooperation between the relevant industry sectors was also evaluated (codes of conduct, common standards for rating systems, promotion of PICS). Possible user awareness and media education measures are also put forward for debate.

The Green Paper identified a series of questions for further debate on issues the Commission considered important in order to define future policy actions. These included:

Question 1

Taking account of what is technically feasible and economically reasonable, what should be the liability of different operators in the content communication chain, from the content creator to the final user? What types of liability: penal, civil and editorial should come into play and under what conditions should liability be limited?

Question 2

How should the test of proportionality of any restrictive measures be applied? Inter alia, should any arbitration or conciliation mechanisms at European Union level be envisaged? If so, what sort of mechanisms?

Question 3

How do we determine the right balance between protection of privacy (including allowing users to maintain anonymity on the networks) and the need to enforce liability for illegal behaviour?

Question 4

Should one give priority to a regulatory or a self-regulatory approach (possibly backed up by legislation in the latter case) as regards parental control systems? What measures would be required, inter alia at the European Union level?

Question 5

In what cases should systematic supply of parental control systems be envisaged (according to service type or other criteria)? Should any obligatory regime be envisaged? If so, in what format and to which operators should it apply? What are the essential functions that such systems should provide?

Question 6

How can decentralisation of content rating be implemented, catering for the need to respect individual, local and national sensitivities, where audio-visual and information services are transnational?

Question 7

What elements of standardisation would allow content ratings to be developed in a coherent way in Europe, in particular in the case of digital services (standardisation of types of information to be supplied, of encoding and decoding of such information, etc.)?

Question 8

In what ways should administrative cooperation be implemented in the European Union? How and in what institutional framework should it be formalised?

Question 9

What should the priorities be at the European level and at the international level? In particular, should one give priority to developing solutions at the European Union level and then promoting them at the international level or should this be done in parallel? What are the most appropriate international fora for international cooperation (G7, DECD, ITU, WTD UN or bilateral relations)? How should this international cooperation be formalised?

In its communication from the Commission [2] to the Council, the European Parliament, the Economic and Social Committee and the Committee of the Regions on Illegal and harmful content on the Internet, the Commission recalls that illegal content relates to wider issues than child pornography.

- national security (instructions on bomb-making, illegal drug production and terrorist activities);
- protection of minors (abusive forms of marketing, violence and pornography);
- protection of human dignity (incitement to racial hatred or racial discrimination);
- economic security (fraud and instructions on pirating credit cards);
- information security (malicious hacking);
- protection of privacy (unauthorised communication of personal data and electronic harassment);
- protection of reputation (libel, unlawful comparative advertising); and
- intellectual property (unauthorised distribution of copyrighted works: for example, software or music).

The Internet was recognised as a symbol and had established itself as one of the main drivers of the convergence between telecommunications, computer and content industries. The Internet had also established itself as one of the main building blocks of the Global Information Infrastructure and as an essential enabler of the Information Society in Europe. Characterised by a growth rate unprecedented in the history of communication technologies, at the time of the Communication, the Internet had reached almost 60 million users in 160 countries and was doubling each year. The most popular application, the World Wide Web, based on protocols developed in Europe, was fast becoming a standard vehicle for information publication and electronic commerce, with an estimated 10 million sites worldwide in 1995, up 1600 % over the previous year.

As regards the distribution of illegal content on the Internet, it was clearly the responsibility of Member States to ensure the application of existing laws. What was illegal offline remains illegal online. Harmful content was defined as "both content which is allowed but whose distribution is restricted (adults only, for instance) and content which may offend certain users, although its publication is not restricted because of the principle of freedom of expression". It is interesting to note that Internet issues were still considered as an extension of real-life crime and there was little attention given to new crimes facilitated by the Internet. It was also considered that the presence of illegal and harmful content on the Internet had "direct repercussions on tile workings of the Internal Market In particular, the adoption by Member States of regulations of new Internet services intended to protect the public interest may also create risks of distortions of competition (for example, through widely divergent responses to the question of potential liability of Internet service providers), hamper the free circulation of these services, and lead to a re-fragmentation of the Internal Market."

A conference organised by the Association of London Government ("ALG") called the First European Conference on Combating Violence and Pornography on the Internet was hosted on **13–14 February 1997** [3].[9] The conference was organised to look at what could be done to combat violence and pornography on the

---

[9]http://www2.warwick.ac.uk/fac/soc/law/elj/jilt/1997_1/akdeniz2/ (last accessed 7 Dec 2014).

Internet. The aim of the conference was to focus on the technical and moral issues around policing, legality and censorship to tackle the growing amount of and ever easier access to violence and pornography on the Internet. The conference aimed to influence European policy on tackling violence and pornography on the Internet. Mr. David Kerr stated that in December 1996, there were 28 reports from the online users which resulted in 5 pictures being removed from the UK ISP servers (mainly newsgroups). In January 1997, the Internet Watch Foundation had reported over 100 illegal items to the UK Police and there have been 50 additional reports by online users. Mr Kerr stated that most of the illegal contents on the Internet containing child pornography are posted from outside the UK and the EU (mainly from the USA) and international cooperation is needed to be effective.

According to a report written by Yaman Akdeniz[10] about the conference, Mr. Jorg Tauss, a member of the German Bundestag Committee of Enquiry into Media and Violence, stated that he was against the policing of the Internet for pornography since it is widely available in the streets in his country. Mr. Tauss mentioned the difficulties in defining the word "pornography" and stated that this would be even more complicated in an international environment such as the Internet. While regulation of pornography would be difficult and unworkable, child pornography is a different issue. Mr. Tauss stated that the "Internet is not an illegal vacuum or beyond the rule of law" and that the police should take action to combat child pornography. Mr. Tauss also mentioned that the authorities do not understand the Internet at all and highlighted one case in Germany where the person who had reported child pornography to German authorities was himself prosecuted (because he had the material in his cache memory).

Whereas Sect. 1.3.1 noted that the whole development of the Internet was dominated by commercial interests and market forces and followed the principle of imposing no regulation for the sake of faster development, this was beginning to change. Rapid evolution of Internet services was still supported and encouraged, but it now needed to be supported by a self-regulatory, effective response to clearly articulated Internet concerns. In the early days, the concerns centred on bandwidth (spam and newsgroups) and on child protection, and sometimes these issues combined with the challenge of spam advertising child pornography websites.

Mr. David Kerr[11] was the first Chief Executive of the Internet Watch Foundation and company secretary, Internet Content Rating Association. He was appointed to the IWF in October 1996 to set up and run the organisation, and he was involved in developing public–private partnerships addressing issues such as race relations and rural services. He was appointed to IWF to implement an agreement between the UK Internet industry, government and the police. He was responsible for developing one of the world's first hotlines for dealing with illegal net content with the support of the UK government, police and ISPs. He also played a leading role in specifying a UK rating system and in promoting the development of an

---

[10]Ibid.

[11]http://www.theguardian.com/technology/2000/apr/20/freespeech2 (last accessed 5 Dec 2014).

internationally acceptable rating and filtering scheme. He has led the INCORE project commissioned by the EU to make recommendations on the approach to rating and filtering from a European perspective, which is reporting in mid-2000. The ICRA, a not-for-profit consortium of global net players, was set up to deliver an international rating system. Later in 1999, he participated in the experts network set up by the Bertelsmann Foundation to consider issues of self-regulation of Internet content, which made recommendations to the Internet Content Summit in Munich in September 1999 and was jointly run by the INCORE.

UK ISPs were not present to discuss the availability of pornographic content on the Internet while their potential liability was discussed. Various ideas about self-regulation were discussed and the debate focused on the challenge of self-regulation and how self-regulatory solutions would operate and be effective (Internet Watch Foundation or rating systems such as PICS and RSACi). The main people concerned about the regulation of the Internet were non-users of the Internet.

On **17 February 1997**, the council of the representatives of the governments of the member states [4] adopted a resolution on illegal and harmful content on the Internet (97/C 70/01) and stressed the importance of three action projects:

- encourage and facilitate self-regulatory systems including representative bodies for Internet service providers and users, effective codes of conduct and possibly hotline reporting mechanisms available to the public;
- encourage the provision to users of filtering mechanisms and the setting up of rating systems; for example the PICS (platform for Internet content selection) standard launched by the international World Wide Web consortium with Community support should be promoted;
- participate actively in the International Ministerial Conference to be hosted by Germany and encourage attendance by representatives of the actors concerned.

2.2.6 US Framework for Global Electronic Commerce

On 1 July 1997, the US government published a document on a Framework for Global Electronic Commerce (Clinton and Gore [5].[12] President William J. Clinton and Vice President Albert Gore, Jr. wrote that "*the Internet is being used to reinvent government and reshape our lives and our communities in the process. As the Internet empowers citizens and democratizes societies, it is also changing classic business and economic paradigms. New models of commercial interaction are developing as businesses and consumers participate in the electronic marketplace and reap the resultant benefits. Entrepreneurs are able to start new businesses more easily, with smaller up-front investment requirements*". They went on to say

---

[12]The Global Information Infrastructure (GII)—The Framework. http://clinton4.nara.gov/WH/New/Commerce/read.html (last accessed 8 Dec 2014).

that "Governments can have a profound effect on the growth of commerce on the Internet. By their actions, they can facilitate electronic trade or inhibit it". Principles of the framework include the following:

1. The private sector should lead. Innovation, expanded services, broader participation and lower prices will arise in a market-driven arena, not in an environment that operates as a regulated industry.
2. Governments should avoid undue restrictions on electronic commerce. Business models must evolve rapidly to keep pace with the breakneck speed of change in the technology; government attempts to regulate are likely to be outmoded by the time they are finally enacted.
3. Where governmental involvement is needed, its aim should be to support and enforce a predictable, minimalist, consistent and simple legal environment for commerce. Its goal should be to ensure competition, protect intellectual property and privacy, prevent fraud, foster transparency, support commercial transactions and facilitate dispute resolution.
4. Governments should recognise the unique qualities of the Internet. We should not assume, for example, that the regulatory frameworks established over the past sixty years for telecommunications, radio and television fit the Internet. Regulation should be imposed only as a necessary means to achieve an important goal on which there is a broad consensus. Existing laws and regulations that may hinder electronic commerce should be reviewed and revised or eliminated to reflect the needs of the new electronic age.
5. Electronic Commerce over the Internet should be facilitated on a global basis. The legal framework supporting commercial transactions on the Internet should be governed by consistent principles across state, national and international borders that lead to predictable results regardless of the jurisdiction in which a particular buyer or seller resides.

The framework identified that the goal was to ensure that online service providers can reach end-users on reasonable and non-discriminatory terms and condition, and there were several areas of concern such as access to leased lines, local loops pricing, interconnection and unbundling and attaching equipment to the network. Bilateral exchanges with individual foreign governments, regional fora such as APEC and CITEL, and multilateral fora such as the OECD and ITU, and various other fora (i.e. international alliances of private businesses, the International Organization of Standardization [ISO], the International Electrotechnical Commission [IEC]), also were used for international discussions on telecommunication-related Internet issues and removing trade barriers that inhibit the export of information technology. These issues include the terms and conditions governing the exchange of online traffic, addressing and reliability.

In the area of online content, four areas of concern were listed as follows:

1. Regulation of content,
2. Foreign content quotas,
3. Regulation of advertising,
4. Regulation to prevent fraud.

The Administration encouraged the creation of private fora to take the lead in areas requiring self-regulation such as privacy, content ratings and consumer protection and in areas such as standards development, commercial code and fostering interoperability.

It is clear that the focus of the US strategy was to encourage information society services and Internet growth, and there was very little consideration of the downside issues of the Internet such as emerging cybercrime trends. The conflict between responding to illegal and harmful content and supporting and encouraging Internet services became a major challenge in Europe.

Section 1.2 identified the problem of blurring boundaries which further contributed to the uncertainty as to who and how cybersecurity would be governed. It was not clear what the applicable legal and regulatory regimes were and which roles private stakeholders would play in safeguarding cyberspace. These framework papers, Green Papers and the European conferences started the debate to tease out the potential for safeguarding cyberspace and to identify the legitimate and reasonable roles of the variety of stakeholders. More importantly, it sought to identify the realistic limits of regulation, self-regulation and co-regulation in the new world of cyberspace.

2.2.7 Global Information Networks: Realising the Potential Conference, Bonn Germany

The Federal Republic of Germany and the European Commission jointly organised the European Ministerial Conference entitled "Global Information Networks: Realising the Potential", held in Bonn from **6–8 July 1997** [6].[13] Ministers from the Member States of the European Union, members of the European Free Trade Association and countries of the Central and Eastern Europe and Cyprus, members of the European Commission, guests from the USA, Canada, Japan and Russia and representatives from industry, users and European and international organisations attended the Conference. Ministers recognised the key role which the private sector is playing in the emergence of Global Information Networks, in particular through investments in infrastructures and services. They considered that the expansion of Global Information Networks must essentially be market-led and left to private

---

[13]http://web.mclink.it/MC8216/netmark/attach/bonn_en.htm#Heading01 (last accessed 7 Dec 2014).

initiative. They believe that private enterprise should drive the expansion of electronic commerce in Europe. Ministers also agreed that any regulatory framework for electronic commerce should be clear and predictable, pro-competitive, strike the right balance between the freedom of expression and the protection of private and public interests, in particular the protection of minors, and ensure consumer protection.

Ministers declared the emergence of Global Information Networks as a highly positive development. They considered this to be of crucial importance for Europe's future and an opportunity for all, businesses small and large, citizens and public administrations. They stressed the special characteristics and fundamentally transnational nature of the Internet which set it apart in almost every way from the then traditional means of communication. Ministers recognised that these new opportunities come with new challenges and that the sheer pace of development could have created technological and legal uncertainties. Such concerns, if not addressed, would delay investments by businesses and slow down take-up by users.

Ministers noted with satisfaction the key role taken by the industry itself in the process of standards setting. They considered that technological and commercial interoperability in a competitive environment was a vital factor for the development of Global Information Networks. Ministers recognised that it was crucial to build trust and confidence in Global Information Networks by ensuring that basic human rights were respected and by safeguarding the interests of society in general, including producers and consumers, particularly through fair and transparent offers of service. This could be achieved by protection of creativity and investment, security and confidentiality, digital signatures and responsibility of the actors.

The most important policy decision by Europe in the evolving area of self-regulation was made during this conference and the subsequent Ministerial declaration. Ministers stressed that the rules on responsibility for content should be based on a set of common principles so as to ensure a level playing field. Therefore, intermediaries such as network operators and access providers should, in general, not be responsible for content. This principle should be applied in such a way that intermediaries such as network operators and access providers are not subject to unreasonable, disproportionate or discriminatory rules. In any case, third-party content hosting services should not be expected to exercise prior control on the content which they have no reason to believe is illegal. Due account should be taken of whether such intermediaries had reasonable grounds to know and reasonable possibility to control the content. Ministers considered that rules on responsibility should give effect to the principle of freedom of speech, respect public and private interests and not impose disproportionate burdens on actors.

As noted in Chap. 1, when the government has no agenda for promoting and supporting self-regulation [...], the private sector itself can be very sceptical about self-regulation or initiatives may be undermined by state apathy towards lack of driving forces and uncertainty of, current legal statutes.

2.2.8 Irish Working Group on Illegal and Harmful Use of the Internet

In Dublin, in **March 1997**, I had a meeting with Mr. Colm Greely, well known for his time in Ireland Online (the first consumer-focused Internet service provider in Ireland). As a senior manager in Ireland Online and very knowledgeable on the Internet, he had been approached by the Irish Department of Justice, Equality and Law Reform about his participation on a committee assessing the impact of the Internet. He attended a few meetings and then decided he would approach me to determine if I would get involved with the project. We knew each other throughout my time in IEunet and respected the work we had both done. He explained to me that this new committee was created to investigate and make recommendations about the illegal and harmful use of the Internet. He was interested in the area, but his commitments to Ireland Online were significant, and more importantly, he was being asked to participate in the committee as an overall unbiased industry representative and not only as a representative of Ireland Online. Ireland Online was then working very closely with Postgem, which was a subsidiary of An Post and was in direct competition with Telecom Eireann. He described the individual participants in the committee on the illegal and harmful use of the Internet who were from a range of different sectors from Film Censorship, An Garda Siochana, Department of Enterprise and Employment, Department of Justice, Equality and Law Reform, Department of Foreign Affairs, Department of Finance, Department of Education, UNICEF, Department of Health and Children and Department of Communications, University College Cork, the University of Limerick and Ireland Online. For many of these participants, they had very basic knowledge of the Internet, how the Internet functioned, Internet services, Internet companies or stakeholders in the Irish market. The committee was chaired by Mr. John Haskins from the Department of Justice, Equality and Law Reform and was working through their terms of reference and developing a work plan for the committee meetings and the creation of targeted themed subgroups.

Colm suggested that I should take over his role as a broader industry representative in the committee since I knew most about the Internet services available in Ireland today and personally knew each of the Internet organisations, their management and many of their staff. I had managed to maintain their respect throughout my time in IEunet. He felt that it was too complex for him to represent the interests of his company while at the same time to represent the views of the wider Internet marketplace in Ireland. While he could make a reasonably fair attempt at achieving this balance, there was no forum for him to meet with competitors in the market and ask their views on a range of subjects in order to represent those views during meetings of the committee on illegal and harmful use of the Internet. Like Colm Greely, I could probably accurately estimate the views of the Internet service providers on a range of social, political and business issues, but I also understood that the open nature of this government committee meant it had the ability to move in a range of complex and diverse directions which would challenge the limits of my experiences or knowledge. However, I would be able to meet with each of the industry players and could probably be accepted as a fair broker and representative of those views with no personal/professional agenda being in play. I therefore agreed to take on the role and started working on the committee from the next meeting.

The Working Group on Illegal and Harmful Use of the Internet [7] was created at a time when "the Internet still represents a vague concept to many people. Understandably, they find it difficult to grasp the idea of a network-of-networks-of-computers which has no central ownership, is almost indestructible and is growing at an unknowable rate".

The terms of reference of the Working Group were guided by the European Commission that published a Green Paper on the Protection of Minors and Human Dignity in Audio-Visual and Information Services published on 16 October 1996. The terms of reference were to identify the nature and extent of the issues surrounding the illegal and harmful use of the Internet; to prioritise such issues with particular reference to the need to address the issue of child pornography in the short term; and to examine and assess the current approaches both domestically and internationally to addressing the problem of the illegal and harmful use of the Internet, in relation to those issues that can be domestically addressed, to identify the legal, technical and structural problems that arise; and to make specific recommendations for their resolution in the short, medium and long term as appropriate, in relation to those issues that require resolution in an international context, to make recommendations which will inform policy in this regard.

"In its mandate to examine the illegal and harmful use of the Internet, the Group was continually conscious of the need for balance in its treatment of the subject matter. The Internet allows the same ease of expression to evil as it does to good. In fact, it can be argued that with its relative anonymity and global dimensions, it facilitates the full expression of our darker side more than any other communication medium so far." The inaugural meeting of the Group took place on 25 February 1997 and the deliberations of the Group extended over a period of 11 months. A total of 13 plenary sessions were held. Four subgroups covering Legal implications, International aspects, Child issues, and Issues relating to the role of Internet service providers (ISPs) also had several meetings, and 47 written submissions were received. The Group also heard a further 6 detailed oral presentations. Based on their particular experience in the area of combating child pornography on the Internet, Mr. David Kerr of Internet Watch Foundation (UK) and Mr. Nigel Williams of Childnet International were also invited to address the Group.

Mr. Nigel Williams[14] (died 26 March 2006) was a native of Northern Ireland and the founder of the London-based charity Childnet International and had an international reputation for his work on the impact of the Internet on children. (In 2003, he was appointed as Northern Ireland's first commissioner for children.) A significant part of his work with Childnet (established 1995), while working in

---

[14]http://www.theguardian.com/society/2006/mar/31/childrensservices.northernireland (last accessed 5 Dec 2014).

Westminster as head of public policy for Christian Action Research and Education (CARE), concerned pornography. He recognised the need to protect children from danger and published a book on the subject, False Images. Overall, however, he was clear that what information technology offered was essentially positive. Parents needed to recognise that their children would benefit from what he called this "parallel universe". He was also a board member of the Internet Watch Foundation and the Internet Content Rating Association, and in 2001, it was appointed to the home secretary's task force on child protection on the Internet.

The period from 1996 to 1998 was an amazing period in the evolution of self-regulation. The methodology adopted offered a focused structured process to identify the essential issues relating to Internet technologies and the diverse services evolving from their widespread adoption. A number of the working group members were quite knowledgeable on the subject area, but there were also quite a few who had very limited understanding of the operation of the Internet, the range of different organisations responsible for effective Internet operation and the different levels of knowledge and capabilities of these organisations in any effective self-regulatory response. In addition, the range of illegal activities and harmful activities possible was identified and the difference between current criminal activities in the real world and online crime was debated. It was a very thought provoking process. These areas are highlighted in Fig. 2.1.

As an Internet technology expert, I was respected by all members of the working group. As a person representing the interests of the wider Internet industry, my opinion was treated with suspicion and assumed to be focused on the short-term

National security:
- Terrorist activities
- Instructions on bomb making
- Hacking into government computer networks

Injury to children
- Child pornography
- Adult pornography
- Material depicting extreme violence
- Child trafficking
- Advice on anonymous exchange of graphic material

Injury to human dignity
- Racial discrimination, incitement to racial hatred
- Extreme sexual perversion

Economic security
- All types of fraud
- Instructions on credit card piracy

Information security
- Malicious hacking

Privacy protection
- Unauthorised mailing
- Interception of personal e-mail
- Misuse of personal data
- Unfair obtaining of personal data

Protection of reputation
- Libel

Gambling

Information on or sale of "controlled drugs"

Intellectual property
- Copyright infringements of any medium
- Unauthorised distribution of videos, music, software etc.

Fig. 2.1 1998 Sect. 1.3.1 First Report of Illegal and Harmful use of the Internet—the concept of illegal use of the Internet covers a wide range of subject matter under a diverse range of identified categories

narrow interests of the industry. It was a challenging period to share my knowledge of Internet systems and the low level of cooperation and sharing between the different industry players. Whereas the early interests of the working group were to understand the detailed inner workings of networked computer systems and the Internet in particular, the emphasis on gaining a deeper understanding on the range of Internet services, protocols and the international nature of Internet activities was of immense importance. At times, it seemed that the range of issues would over-whelm the aims and objectives of the committee.

To support this process, documents were prepared describing the structure of the industry and the layers of interconnectivity at the organisational level. These documents described the level of visibility these players had at different levels in the technology network models. It is necessary to understand the various players in the industry and their role in relation to the carrying, processing and storage of information on its journey throughout the Internet. The roles can be broken into seven main areas including the consumer groups (Individuals, Families, companies, Research Organisations, Universities, Schools, Government Agencies, Employees, Students, etc.), the telecommunications circuit provider, the Internet access provider (including TCP/IP address allocation, domain name registration, dial-in facilities, email, newsgroup and the web services), the facilities providers (include hosting and web farm), the content providers, the broadcasters and the regulatory agencies. For example, the role of a Domain Registry both at the country level and at the global level was described in detail. Prepared documents described the different Internet services being sold, how they are implemented and the possibilities of interception and disruption of illegal and harmful activities. Section 1.5.3 of the proposed NIS directive [8] indicates out these categories have continued to increase including a greater number of industry stakeholders including e-commerce plat-forms, Internet Payment gateways, social networks, cloud computing services and application stores. These were later increased to include Internet exchange points, national domain name registries and the web hosting services.

An alternative method of describing the roles is to do so in terms of the elec-tronic services provided including electronic mail, network news, web browsing, web provision, online chat, file transfer and other services. (Note that Social Net-working Services had not started operating yet.) I described the potential options the different stakeholders could implement in combating illegal and harmful content. The data travelling across the ISP network operations centre (backbone) are pro-cessed automatically and unless deliberately intercepted are never seen, heard or read by human operators. The sheer volume and complexity negated any reasonable analysis without prior knowledge and specific targeting of potential abuse.

2.2.9 Electronic Mail

Email allows the exchange of messages and documents in a one-to-one and one-to-many manner. These messages are usually plain text, but attached files can be graphics, spreadsheets, reports, etc. It is also possible to encrypt email content to prevent others from intercepting it. Email can be particularly difficult to regulate since the messages can be considered as communication between parties with entitlements to privacy and confidentiality. The communication can be encrypted preventing interception and therefore regulation. One aspect of email activity which can be regulated is that of "spamming"—a process where volume email is targeted at end-users without their request—in essence "junk" mail.

2.2.10 Newsgroups

The newsgroups are spread across 15,000 different topics, and in theory, it is possible to prevent the distribution of specific newsgroups. However, there is no technical method of controlling the content of any newsgroup—it is subject to self-regulation and net etiquette. The blocking of specific newsgroups is feasible but cannot be considered as a definitive solution to illegal or harmful content. It is possible for users to inject news messages into the news system using international news hosts, thus bypassing local regulations In addition, users can read the news database stored on international servers which would have a significant impact on international bandwidth if large numbers were to adopt this approach.

2.2.11 Web Browsing

Web browsing allowed end-users to use Microsoft Internet Explorer[15] or Netscape Navigator[16] from Netscape to browse information in a graphical and hierarchical manner on remote servers located in all countries of the world. This content could span the full range of work-related research material, edutainment for home education to illegal and harmful material. The wide range of dubious material has created real concerns among many Internet users. Its success continues to grow and newer technologies will enable faster and wider distribution of the web content. The recent standards in relation to PICS[17] (Platform for Internet Content Selection) allow substantial choice in the categorisation of website content. Browsing software now checks each site selected for a site rating hosted on a separate server for the style and content of the selected site. Simple rules can permit or deny access to sites

---

[15]Microsoft originally released Internet Explorer 1.0 in August 1995.

[16]Netscape Navigator 1.0 initial release was on 15 December 1994.

[17]http://www.w3.org/PICS/ (last accessed 8 Dec 2014). The PICS specification enables labels (metadata) to be associated with Internet content. It was originally designed to help parents and teachers control what children access on the Internet, but it also facilitates other uses for labels, including code signing and privacy. The PICS platform is one on which other rating services and filtering software have been built. PICS has been superseded by the Protocol for Web Description Resources (POWDER).

based on criteria specified by the parent, manager or users themselves. In addition, end-users and institutions would want rating agencies particularly tuned to their ethos and responsibilities.

2.2.12 Web Hosting

Websites could be hosted anywhere in the world, and a single site can even span multi-jurisdictional boundaries. The site can contain text, graphics, video clips, music and sound clips in addition to more complex interfaces to remote databases which can be located in different geographical boundaries.

2.2.13 File Transfer

File transfer permitted the copying of documents, graphics, video clips and audio clips from any part of the world onto the local computer or from the local computer onto a remote computer system. The file transfer process was normally performed manually by the user, but on many systems could be completely automated. The remote files could be encoded, compressed and even encrypted. Many systems offered anonymous FTP facilities which were essentially a large volume of publicly accessible files available for download by anyone without password access. Some organisations offer controlled (username and password) access to files and documents for a financial charge.

2.2.14 Online Chat

CHAT (not to be mistaken with Voice-over IP—voip which arrived later) was the Internet equivalent of voice chat lines except that the users participating in the forums each type their message which is then copied onto the screen of each participant in the group. The "conversations" could cover a very broad range of subjects including illegal and harmful areas. Many of these discussion groups were publicly advertised and users could specify to their chat software that they are interested in taking part. It is also possible to have closed group discussions by prior arrangement. The primary target of any regulatory activity would be the publicly advertised groups. This would still be a major technical problem since the location of the broadcast point can easily move across international boundaries with ease.

There were several major issues identified which are critical to any conversation or debate on self-regulation. Firstly, there was the issue of the critical and important difference between illegal and harmful content and activity. The report stated that "decisions on acceptability of harmful material are subjective and are very much context-based. There are variations in levels of acceptability not only between countries but also within countries. What some people might find distasteful and offensive, others may not. While the cultural norms may mediate what is considered to be 'acceptable', any form of consensus is, at best, problematic".[18]

The second issue was the recognition that there are significant differences in any effective response to activity- and content-related issues (illegal or harmful).

The third critical issue was the acceptance that the Internet was international in nature and that it would be technically challenging for any single country to adopt and implement a national approach to Internet issues which was not internationally accepted and endorsed. It required international collaboration to be effective.

Much of the work of this group is still relevant today, and although many of the risks identified in this working group have received much attention and disruption as a result of a range of international effective responses, a number of challenges listed in this report remain unresolved. The pace of change on the Internet continues to be phenomenal.

Much of this research was performed *before* Web 2.0 and before social networking services, peer-to-peer software solutions, voice-over-IP (voip) and mobile Internet services were adopted widely. In addition, most users were accessing the Internet over slow-speed links.

2.2.15 Child Pornography

The Irish working group gained a real insight into current research on child pornography on the Internet and the state-of-the-art research being conducted by Prof Max Taylor and Dr. Ethel Quayle in University College Cork. They were researching the increasing production and distribution of child pornographic images on the Internet and created a methodology to grade the type of images into different categories. This work was internationally recognised and created increased awareness and understanding of the increasing risks associated with online crime activity in this area.

2.2.16 Recommendations of the Committee on Illegal and Harmful Use of the Internet

- Self-regulation: A system of self-regulation by the service provider industry should be introduced to include common codes of practice and common acceptable usage conditions.

---

[18]http://www.justice.ie/en/JELR/Pages/Illegal_use_of_the_Internet_report Page 15 (last accessed Dec 14).

- Complaints hotline: A non-statutory national complaints hotline should be established to investigate and process complaints about illegal material on the Internet.
- Advisory Board: A non-statutory advisory board representative of the significant players involved should be established to oversee and coordinate measures aimed at ensuring the success of the self-regulatory framework.
- Awareness: Any national awareness campaigns proposed by the Information Society Commission should include a dimension which addresses the potential for illegal and harmful use of the Internet.
- Other awareness measures should include:

  - An active role for service providers in the education of their clients on the safe use of the Internet.
  - The active involvement of the new hotline and Advisory Group in the development of awareness programmes.
  - The specific targeting of parents and teachers.
  - The incorporation of modules on Internet safety into the curriculum of teachers, care workers, Gardaí, Customs officers and any other agencies who come in contact with issues relating to the downside of the Internet.

- Specific initiatives for schools should include the following:

  - In-career training modules for teachers on Internet issues.
  - The publication of a set of guidelines by the Department of Education and Science for those involved in the Internet in schools.
  - The integration of Internet Ethics into the Curriculum.
  - The staging of information sessions for Parents/Guardians.
  - The development of a Schools Code of Conduct.

- Funding: The initial funding of the hotline should be shared by Government and the service provider industry. The service provider industry should immediately and actively pursue EU funding opportunities which are now available in the area of Internet safety.
- Legislation: New legislation and any reviews of existing legislation should be "Internet proofed" before being submitted to Government for approval.
- Specialist training: Specialist training programmes already begun in the policing area should be urgently pursued and extended to the wider areas of law-enforcement including the judiciary.

2.2.17 Internet Service Provider Associations

A key challenge in the self-regulation area was to have a platform to communicate with the Internet industry. The formation of the ISP associations across Europe and the subsequent representation of the ISP view at government events to promote the views, concerns and interests of the Internet service provider was a critical step forward. The continued development of the ISP associations across Europe and the degree to which they represented the interests and combined energy and resources of all providers was critical to the successful implementation of self-regulation. This was a period of much market upheaval and the composition and ownership of the Internet service providers went through significant change during these years; this continued to evolve as the Internet market developed.

EuroISPA[19] is a pan-European association of European Internet Services Providers Associations (ISPAs). It is the world's largest association of Internet service providers (ISPs), representing over 2300 ISPs across the EU and EFTA countries—including ISPs from Austria, Belgium, the Czech Republic, Finland, France, Germany, Ireland, Italy, Norway, Romania and the UK. The association was established in 1997 to represent the European ISP industry on EU policy and legislative issues and to facilitate the exchange of best practices between national ISP associations. Its secretariat is located in Brussels. EuroISPA is recognised as the voice of the EU ISP industry and is the largest "umbrella" association of Internet service providers in the world. The reason for EuroISPA reflects the views of ISPs of all sizes from across its member base. EuroISPA has signed Memoranda of Understanding with the following organisations: APIA—Asia & Pacific Internet Association; APJII—Indonesian Internet Service Provider Association; CAIP—Canadian Association of Internet Providers; CENTR—Council of European National Top Level Domain Registries; ECOMLAC—Latin America and Caribbean Federation for Internet and Electronic Commerce; HKISPA—Hong Kong Internet Service Providers Association; IIA—Australian Internet Industry Association; INHOPE—The Association of Internet Hotline Providers in Europe; ISPA SA—Internet Service Providers Association South Africa; TELESA—Telecom Services Association, Japan; and US ISPA—United States Internet Service Provider Association.

ECO[20]—The Association of the German Internet Industry, was founded in 1995, has almost 800 member organisations and is the largest Internet industry association in Europe. ECO has been instrumental in the development of the Internet in Germany, fostering new technologies, infrastructures and markets, and forming framework conditions. One of the most important tasks is to represent the interests of ECO members in politics, and in national and international committees. ECO is a member of EuroISPA.

The UK Internet Service Providers' Association (ISPA)[21] was established on 8 August 1997 and is the UK's Trade Association for providers of Internet services. ISPA promotes collaboration and constructive dialogue between its members and the wider Internet community. Companies who choose to become members of ISPA agree to abide by the ISPA UK Code of Practice which was adopted on 25

---

[19]www.euroispa.org (last accessed 8 December 2014).

[20]https://international.eco.de/about.html (last accessed 8 Dec 2014).

[21]http://www.ispa.org.uk/about-us/ispas-industry-role/ (last accessed on 8 Dec 2014).

January 1999. Allegiance to the code means that consumers can view the ISPA UK logo as a mark of commitment to good business practice. ISPA UK was instrumental in founding the Internet Watch Foundation, the UK hotline for reporting illegal online content in 1997 and holds permanent membership. As one of the many funding organisations of the IWF, along with many other ISPA members, ISPA sits on the funding council. The success of the IWF and self-regulation has seen the amount of child abuse images hosted in the UK fall from 18 % in 1997 to less than 0.1 %.

The main Irish service providers formed the Internet Service Providers Association of Ireland (ISPAI) in April 1997. On 5 May 1998, the Internet Service Providers' Association of Ireland[22] was formally registered as a not-for-profit company limited by guarantee of its members, under Company Number 285632. The Association provides one voice for the Irish ISP Industry at the National, International and EU levels. The ISPAI, among other responsibilities, maintains a Code of Practice and Ethics recognised as a role model in the EU and operates a fully functioning and efficient Internet Hotline Service. ISPs agree to adhere to the Code of Practice and Ethics when they become members of the ISPAI.

2.2.18 Bertelsmann Foundation

In **September 1999**, the Bertelsmann Foundation project "Self-Regulation of Internet Content" (Bertelsmann 1999) produced a report which dealt with the problem of harmful and illegal content and the protection of minors on the Internet. Starting from the assumption that no nation state, no major Internet industry player, nor any law enforcement authority could handle this complex task on its own, the project took a coordinated approach in four areas:

- Self-regulation and the Internet industry

  - Only such a systematic approach—bringing technological potential together with the energies and capacities of government, the Internet industry and the citizenry—has the promise of success in meeting what often seem to be competing goals.
  - As part of the codes of conduct, Internet providers hosting content have an obligation to remove illegal content when put on notice that such content exists. The procedure for such notice and takedown—while laid down by regulation—should be reflected in codes of conduct and should specify the requirements for proper notification of service providers.

- Self-rating and filtering
- Hotlines as a feedback mechanism for users
- Law enforcement and the role of legal provisions in supporting self-regulation.

---

[22]http://www.ispai.ie/about/ (last accessed 8 Dec 2014).

It offered 12 recommendations:

- The Internet: changing the way people live
- Self-regulation of Internet content: towards a systematic, integrated and international approach
- Internet industry: developing and implementing codes of conduct
- Sharing responsibility: self-regulatory agencies enforcing codes of conduct
- Governments: supporting and reinforcing self-regulation
- Self-rating and filtering systems: empowering user choice
- Internet filtering: ensuring youth protection and freedom of speech
- Hotlines: communicating and evaluating content concerns
- International cooperation: acting against content where it is located
- The legal framework: limitations on liability
- Law enforcement: cooperation and continuous training
- A "learning system": education and constant evaluation.

2.2.19 EC Daphne Programme

The INHOPE Forum was established in 1998 with financial assistance from the 1997 Daphne Programme,[23] to bring together hotline initiatives across Europe which were responding to child pornography on the Internet. Hotlines provided an easy point of contact and reporting mechanism for Internet users who come across child pornography. Hotlines evaluated these reports according to their procedures and national legislation, and then link with industry and/or the police to ensure the material was removed and/or subject to enforcement action. The 1997 Daphne project had enabled Internet hotlines to come together for the first time and discuss issues of common concern in a very fast-moving environment. This project was undertaken by Childnet International in conjunction with the members of the INHOPE Forum including Austria—ISPA, Finland—Mannerheim League for Child Welfare, France—AFA, Germany—Eco-Forum; FSM; and Jugendschutz.net, Ireland—ISPA Ireland and Norway—Redd Barne. It was supported by the National Center for Missing and Exploited Children in the USA.

In 1999, there were three international conferences that addressed the issue of child pornography on the Internet which are listed below:

- the UNESCO conference in Paris in 18–19 January 1999 was a meeting of experts entitled Sexual Abuse of Children, Child Pornography and Paedophilia on the Internet: an International Challenge [9]. In the framework of the United Nations Convention on the Rights of the Child, this initiative aimed to "alert world opinion to the need to fight child pornography, to combat sexual abuse of

---

[23]http://ec.europa.eu/justice_home/daphnetoolkit/html/projects/dpt_1998_045_c_en.html   (last accessed 8 Dec 2014).

children resulting from the misuse of the Internet, and the mobilisation of human, technical and financial resources to support the work of professionals and non-governmental organisations in the protection of children and to safe-guard their rights in the media and on the Internet"; UNESCO created a website called INNOCENCE IN DANGER[24] and convened a conference, involving over 300 delegates, to discuss

- The sexual abuse of children: family, social and economic context: origins, causes, prevention and care;
- Combating sexual abuse of children: role of civil society;
- Legal and judicial aspects; crime detection and law enforcement: crime detection and law enforcement, extradition;
- Promoting the free flow of information in the face of worldwide concern about the sexual abuse of children, child pornography and paedophilia on the Internet;
- Civil liberties, privacy and Internet abusers; making the Net safe for young children—content providers, spam filters, search engines, self-rating of websites, monitoring and networking;
- Research, information and monitoring sensitisation of the public.

• the Bertelsmann Foundation conference in Munich in September 1999 also addressed wider issues of Internet content and Internet rating. The results of this conference are outlined in the previous section.

• the International Conference on Combatting Child Pornography on the Internet was jointly sponsored by the EU, US Government and Austrian Government on 29 September to 1 October 1999. It was organised by Austrian Foreign Minister Wolfgang Schuessel and US Secretary of State Madeleine Albright and sup-ported by the European Union. The conference intended to mobilise public opinion and encourage cooperation and coordination between judicial and industry authorities. Senior representatives from European and US justice and interior ministries participated with others from the United Nations, the Euro-pean Commission, non-governmental organisations and Internet companies. A network of child pornography operating on the Internet was broken up in August in Vienna and Linz, central Austria, as police arrested three people, including a Catholic priest.[25] The objectives of the conference were to reinforce cooperation among law enforcement officials and the judiciary; to re-establish voluntary self-regulatory mechanisms (codes of conduct) among Internet service providers; and to encourage the establishment of further hotlines (hotlines enable citizens to report leads on child pornography found on the Internet) and of networking among existing hotlines.

The work of the INHOPE Forum complemented these large events by bringing together the specialist group of hotlines dealing with child pornography on the

---

[24]http://www.unesco.org/bpi/eng/unescopress/1999/99-219e.shtml (last accessed 9 Dec 2014).

[25]http://www.cyber-rights.org/reports/interdev.htm (last accessed 9 Dec 2014).

Internet on a day-to-day basis. The work of the INHOPE Forum and the three conferences in 1999 were the foundation of the EC Safer Internet Action Plan. This was also the beginning of the link between child protection issues as an inherent element of Internet self-regulation.

2.2.20 EC Safer Internet Action Plan

On 26 November 1997, a Communication from the Commission to the European Parliament, the Council, the Economic and Social Committee and the Committee of the Regions Action Plan on promoting safe use of the Internet proposal for a council decision adopting a Multiannual Community Action Plan on promoting safe use of the Internet was proposed. The action plan proposed in the communication was described as an important element to combat illegal and harmful content on the Internet. To be effective, it would be closely coordinated with other initiatives in the area of illegal and harmful content, and it would build a bridge to the growing cooperation between police and judicial authorities under the third pillar.

The intense activity of the European institutions in this area since 1996, the political direction given by the European Parliament 2 and the Council, the Ministerial Declaration resulting from the Bonn Conference and the developments in Member States demonstrated that Europe had in many respects been a pioneer in addressing the issues and proposing solutions based on industry self-regulation, filtering and rating, and increasing user confidence through awareness.

The Commission identified areas where concrete measures are needed and where community resources should be made available in order to encourage an environment favourable to the development of the Internet industry:

- promotion of self-regulation and creation of content-monitoring schemes including an European network of hotlines to achieve a high level of protection (especially dealing with content such as child pornography, racism or anti-semitism);
- demonstration and application of effective filtering services and compatible rating systems, which take account of cultural and linguistic diversity; and
- promotion of awareness actions directed at users, in particular children, parents and teachers, to allow them to use Internet resources provided by industry safely and with confidence.

It took two more years for the Commission Communication to become Decision No 276/1999/EC [10] when on 25 January 1999, the European Parliament and of the Council adopted a Multiannual Community Action Plan on promoting safer use of the Internet by combating illegal and harmful content on global networks. It acknowledged that cooperation from the industry in setting up voluntary systems of self-regulation can efficiently help to limit the flow of illegal content on the Internet. The action plan covered the period of four years from 1 January 1999 to 31 December 2002, and the financial framework for the implementation of the plan was set at €25 million. The action plan was later extended [11] until 31 December 2004, and the budget increased by €13.3 million to cover the two extra years.

In summary, it clarified that the distinction between illegal and harmful content is important[26] as these two types of content are dealt with differently:

- illegal content must be dealt with at source by the police and the judicial authorities, whose activities are covered by national legislation and judicial cooperation agreements. However, the industry can be of considerable assistance in restricting the circulation of illegal content (particularly in the case of child pornography, racism and anti-semitism) by means of effective self-regulation schemes (such as codes of conduct and hotlines) governed and supported by legislation, and with consumer backing;
- harmful content is both that which is authorised but has restricted circulation (e.g. for adults only) and content which could be offensive to some users, even if publication is not restricted because of the freedom of speech. Action to combat harmful content first and foremost means developing technology (filtering tools and rating mechanisms) to enable users to reject such content by promoting awareness among parents and fostering self-regulation, which could be an adequate way of protecting minors in particular.

The action plan is divided into four sections:

- establishing a safer environment through a European network of "hotlines" and by encouraging self-regulation and the adoption of codes of conduct;
- developing filtering and rating systems, in particular by highlighting their benefits and facilitating an international agreement on rating systems;
- encouraging awareness campaigns at all levels to inform parents and all people dealing with children (teachers, social workers, etc.) of the best way to protect minors against exposure to content that could be harmful to their development; and
- conducting support activities to assess legal implications, providing coordination with similar international initiatives and assessing the impact of community measures.

On 3 November 2003, there was a Communication from the Commission concerning the evaluation of the Multiannual Community Action Plan [12] on promoting safer use of the Internet and new online technologies by combating illegal and harmful content primarily in the area of the protection of children and minors. The report stressed the positive impact of the action plan, particularly in fostering networking and providing a wealth of information about the problems of safer use of the Internet. In particular, the report concluded that:

- the programme had achieved a good result in producing a number of filtering software products although take-up of rating needed to be increased. Moreover, not all stakeholders agreed that filtering was the best approach to child

---

[26]http://europa.eu/legislation_summaries/information_society/Internet/l24190_en.htm (last accessed 8 Dec 2014).

protection. At the policy level, the programme was successful in putting the issues of developing a safer Internet firmly on the agenda of the EU and the Member States;

- at action-line level, the Commission had instigated the development of a network of hotlines in Europe with associated members in the USA and Australia, funded research into tackling awareness-raising with end-users, stimulated the development of filtering and supported the development of an international rating system; and
- the programme had been successful in linking up stakeholders to produce a "community of actors", although the commission is disappointed by the lack of industry involvement as well as self-regulation organisations and consumer groups.

On 11 May 2005, the Council adopted a Decision establishing the Safer Internet Plus programme [13], to cover the years 2005–2008, aimed at promoting safer use of the Internet and new online technologies. A budget of €45 million was allocated to the programme for the period 2005–2008, and almost 50 % of the budget was allocated for awareness-raising measures. The new programme was geared towards the following activities:

- funding hotlines, so that they could act at national level and cooperate with other centres in the European network of hotlines;
- supporting telephone helplines for children confronted with illegal and harmful content;
- collection of qualitative and quantitative data on the establishment and operation of hotlines;
- launching incentive measures to speed up the process of setting up hotlines and developing codes of conduct; and
- setting up a coordination centre for the network to raise its visibility at European level, improve its operational effectiveness and promote exchanges of information and experience.

The programme provided funding for technological measures which enable users to limit the amount of unwanted and harmful contents and manage the spam they receive. This included:

- assessing the effectiveness of available filtering technology;
- facilitating and coordinating exchanges of information and best practices;
- increasing take-up of content rating and quality-site labels; and
- if necessary, contributing to the accessibility of filter technology, notably in languages not adequately covered by the market.

A fully functioning system of self-regulation was considered to be an essential element in limiting the flow of unwanted, harmful and illegal content. It was considered that self-regulation involved a number of components: consultation and appropriate representation of the parties concerned, codes of conduct, national bodies facilitating cooperation at Community level and national evaluation of self-regulation frameworks. To improve self-regulation in the sector, the Commission provided national co-regulatory or self-regulatory bodies with the Safer Internet Forum as a platform for exchanging experience. The Forum was set up in 2004 under the Safer Internet Action Plan. Its objectives were given as follows:

- to stimulate networking of the appropriate structures within Member States and developing links with self-regulatory bodies outside Europe;
- to stimulate self-regulation on issues such as quality rating of websites, cross-media content rating, rating and filtering techniques, extending them to new forms of content such as online games and new forms of access such as mobile phones;
- to encourage service providers to draw up codes of conduct; and
- to promote research into the effectiveness of rating projects and filtering technologies.

On 5 May 2012, a Communication from the Commission to the European Parliament, the Council, The European Economic and Social Committee and the Committee of the Regions described a European Strategy for a Better Internet for Children. It stated that children have particular needs and vulnerabilities on the Internet, which must be addressed specifically so that the Internet becomes a place of opportunities for children to access knowledge, to communicate, to develop their skills and to improve their job perspectives and employability [14]. The strategy[27] proposed a series of actions grouped around the following main goals:

- stimulate the production of creative and educational online content for children as well as promoting positive online experiences for young children;
- scaling up awareness and empowerment including teaching of digital literacy and online safety in all EU schools;
- create a safe environment for children through age-appropriate privacy settings, wider use of parental controls and age rating and content classification; and
- combat child sexual abuse material online and child sexual exploitation.

2.2.21 The INHOPE (Internet Hotline Providers of Europe) Association

During 1995–1999, various national initiatives brought together the relevant stakeholders to consider how to prevent illegal activity and especially the abuse of children on the Internet. These initiatives were briefly mentioned in Sect. 1.3 which lists the early hotline initiatives.

In Germany, a number of separate initiatives commenced that were first discussed at the time of high-profile court cases and parliamentary debates in 1995/1996. In June 1996, the first Internet child pornography hotline was established in the Netherlands by concerned individuals in the industry and among users, with the

---

[27]Key priorities of the EU e-Skills strategy "e-Skills for the twenty-first century" COM(2007)496.

support of the police. This was quickly followed by initiatives in Norway, Belgium and the UK before the end of 1996. Other countries began to take notice, and plans for hotlines were being finalised in Austria, Ireland, Finland, Spain and France. The issue was extensively debated in other European countries as well. In March 1998, the USA launched its "Cybertipline" which quickly became established as one of the busiest hotlines.

In 1997, the INHOPE Forum was created and 8 hotlines came together to form the INHOPE Association. The hotlines agreed the statutes of the association, and it was formally established as a Dutch company on 23 November 1999. The first executive was elected on that date, and Ms. Ruth Dixon, Assistant Chief Executive of the United Kingdom Internet Watch Foundation, was elected as inaugural President. The organisation continues today and meets regularly to share and exchange knowledge and best practices in the operation of Internet hotlines.

Hotlines must provide a mechanism for receiving complaints from the public about alleged illegal content and/or use of the Internet; they must have effective transparent procedures for dealing with complaints, and they must have the support of government, industry, law enforcement and Internet users in the countries of operation. In addition to these requirements, to be a member of INHOPE, a hotline must cooperate with other members in exchanging information about illegal content, share their expertise, make a commitment to maintain confidentiality and respect the procedures of other members. The purpose of a hotline is to quickly and efficiently remove illegal material from the Internet, to enable a swift investigation by Law Enforcement and to collaborate at the international level with other members of INHOPE.

Each hotline has a strong mandate from the appropriate National Government, Internet Industry, Law Enforcement and Child Welfare. This broad support has been essential to the success achieved so far. There have been many lessons learned during the last two years that were extremely demanding on INHOPE and the individual hotlines. Even though each country has its own individual legislation relating to illegal material on the Internet, the primary focus of the INHOPE association relates to illegal child pornography and online abuse of children. However, some hotlines also deal with illegal adult pornography and/or crimes of xenophobia and racism.

2.2.22 Legislation and Conventions

From the year 2000 onwards, the focus shifted towards regulatory activities with self-regulation evolving towards a multi-stakeholder, co-regulated approach. The Internet industry players were strongly encouraged and motivated through the carrot and stick approach of reasonable legislation supported by threats of draconian regulations in order to continue to support self-regulatory activities. This was very much supported by industry stakeholders who preferred to maintain direct control over their organisations and their ethical stance based on market pressure and customer demands while enabling dynamic business ideas and models to be tested on the Internet.

During the period from 2000 to 2010, there was significant growth of new legislation. In Europe, the focus was on regulation of electronic commerce, online copyright protection, child protection, data protection, data retention and critical infrastructure protection. All these areas required significant participation and commitments from Internet Industry and were set against the background of continually evolving Internet technologies and the global impact of mobile technologies and the arrival of the computer touch screen tablet. This was also the period when social networking and Internet 2.0 later arrived into the mainstream.

2.2.23   Directive 2000/31/EC on Certain Legal Aspects of Information Society Services, in Particular Electronic Commerce

There are two documents of Interest which were significant milestones in the support and encouragement of the Internet industry self-regulation: firstly, directive 2000/31/EC of the European Parliament and of the Council of 8 June 2000 titled on certain legal aspects of information society services, in particular electronic commerce [15] and was one of the cornerstones of self-regulation. Section 2.4 of this directive clearly specified the liability of intermediary service providers through the definition of "mere conduit" for Internet society services, article 13 with the definition of "caching", article 14 with the role of hosting providers and article 15 with the prohibition of a general obligation of monitoring services. These articles were the most important legal specifications in the European sphere to describe the role, responsibilities and limitations of Internet service providers. Article 13 clearly states that the "*service provider is not liable for the information transmitted, on condition that the provider [...] does not select or modify the information contained in the transmission.*" This is explicitly refined in Article 14 that "*Member States shall ensure that the service provider is not liable for the information stored at the request of a recipient of the service, on condition that: (a) the provider does not have actual knowledge of illegal activity or information and, as regards claims for damages, is not aware of facts or circumstances from which the illegal activity or information is apparent; or (b) the provider, upon obtaining such knowledge or awareness, acts expeditiously to remove or to disable access to the information*". Article 16 describes the role of codes of conduct.

2.2.24   The Council of Europe Cybercrime Convention

On 23 November 2001, the Council of Europe Cybercrime convention [16] was opened for signature by the Member States of the Council of Europe and by non-Member States that have participated in its elaboration, in Budapest. It entered into force on 1 July 2004. In November 1996, the European Committee on Crime Problems (CDPC) decided (CDPC/103/211196) to set up a committee of experts to deal with cybercrime. On 4 February 1997 (at the 583rd meeting of the Ministers' Deputies), the Committee of Ministers set up the new committee, called "the Committee of Experts on Crime in Cyber-space (PC-CY)". This Committee PC-CY started its work in April 1997 and undertook negotiations on a draft international convention on cybercrime. Although, under its original terms of reference, the Committee was due to finish its work by 31 December 1999, the document was not completed until December 2000. The text of the convention was developed over the previous years and succinctly specified the challenges of cybercrime and described the preferred roles and responsibilities of the Internet service providers in combating cybercrime. It serves as a guideline for any country developing comprehensive national legislation against cybercrime and as a framework for international cooperation between State Parties to the treaty. The convention was the first international treaty on crimes committed via the Internet and other computer networks, dealing particularly with infringements of copyright, computer-related fraud, child pornography and violations of network security. It also contains a series of powers and procedures such as the search of computer networks and interception. Its main objective is to pursue a common criminal policy aimed at the protection of society against cybercrime, especially by adopting appropriate legislation and fostering international cooperation. For industry stakeholders, the convention created definitions for issues and activities which were in constant debate but rarely agreed and enabled a precise and simple debate to occur in relation to international collaboration on cybercrime issues. In particular, it provided the first internationally agreed definitions on types of crime. It further enabled the debate on traffic data as a separate entity than the content of data communications, which were subject to stricter data protection rules. This later evolved into discussions on traffic meta-data which became subject to data retention and data disclosure legislation and is still debated intensely today. It created understandings on expedited preservation and expedited disclosure including partial disclosure of stored computer data including the need for a national legal context for these activities to take place. There are still significant debates on several issues which were addressed in the convention with special interest in the practical implementation—particularly in the area of search and seizure of stored computer data and interception of content data. Section 32b continues to incur significant debate and disagreement relating to direct access by third countries' law enforcement authorities to data stored in other jurisdiction.[28] The Article 29 working Group[29] identifies the need to obtain the "lawful and voluntary consent of the person who has the lawful authority to disclose the data".

---

[28]http://ec.europa.eu/justice/data-protection/article-29/documentation/other-document/files/2013/ 20131205_wp29_letter_to_cybercrime_committee.pdf (last accessed 10 Jan 2015).

[29]Article 29 Directive 95/46/EC of 24 October 1995 on the protection of individuals with regard to the processing of personal data and on the free movement of such data (OJ L 281, 23.11.1995, p. 31) sets up a Working Party on the Protection of Individuals with regard to the Processing of Personal Data. The "Article 29 Working Party" has advisory status and acts independently.

2.3 Conclusion

Self-regulation and co-regulation are powerful strategies in combining the strengths and expertise of multiple stakeholders against a common concern such as child abuse and xenophobia in a new complex medium such as the Internet or the mobile space. However, it can be dangerous if we do not understand the motivations of the various stakeholders involved in the activity, and it is important to balance the needs of appropriate levels of criminal investigations and crime prevention with human rights, family life and freedom of speech as defined in the Universal Declaration of Human Rights[30] and the European Convention on Human Rights.[31] It is important that these competing rights are balanced to avoid suspicion of a lack of transparency and accountability. This can be achieved through open processes and procedures and ensuring appropriate, relevant external measurements of success. Recent disclosures by Edward Snowden on the activities of the US National Security Agency in widespread monitoring have increased concerns about human rights and about self-regulation over-reach. However, these disclosures have also confused the mandate and the activities of national security agencies globally with the legally approved and transparent activities supporting criminal compliance and criminal investigations for illegal online activities and content.

Self-regulation and co-regulation started at a time when there were few dedicated law enforcement operated cybercrime units globally. However, in the last two decades, every national security and national law enforcement agency has comprehensive, expertly trained, agencies that handle complex cyber investigations with high levels of international collaboration when appropriate. This means that there are greater levels of cooperation between the Internet industry and law enforcement and this activity is supported by the Council of Europe guidelines[32] on this subject. At the European level, the European CyberCrime Centre (EC3) was established in January 2013 and Interpol continues to ramp up its knowledge and expertise in this area.

Chapter 1 notes that cybersecurity is rather a concept or a process than a result, and trust in relationship between government and private sectors is an intangible issue that cannot be simply enforced or imposed by simply implementing mandatory obligations for sharing information about threats.[33] Chapter 1 describes the evolution of self-regulation and co-regulation after 2005 and the increased attempts at direct regulation.

---

[30] http://www.un.org/en/documents/udhr/.

[31] http://www.echr.coe.int/Documents/Convention_ENG.pdf.

[32] http://www.coe.int/t/dghl/cooperation/economiccrime/cybercrime/Documents/LEA_ISP/default_en.asp (last accessed 4 Jan 2015).

[33] Chapter 1, Sect. 1.5.3.

It is reasonable for everyone to debate the nature and style of self-regulation and co-regulation into the future, transparency and accountability requirements and the appropriate balance of cooperation with the role of skilled law enforcement investigations. Otherwise, we will not maintain the trust and support of the Internet users.

Annex—Technology Options: Internet Monitoring and Blocking

Technical solutions for monitoring and blocking have evolved significantly since the beginning of the Internet. There are two main areas of interest including the technical methods of monitoring and blocking and how to specify which content/ user is to be monitored/identified.

A comprehensive approach to monitoring requires both the technology itself (hardware, software and interconnections) and ways to specify/identify the specific content to be blocked or monitored. The nature of the content—image, text, video, voice, etc.—first needs to be determined, and it must be decided whether it is required to log records of traffic data (identities of communicating parties) or record copies of communications (message content) or disrupt the communications flow by either preventing the successful completion of the selected communications or by changing the nature of the communications exchange.

Whereas there are complex methods of protecting traffic from eavesdropping or interception using modern tools for encryption, until recently as a result of the alleged widespread monitoring of Internet traffic directly from the fibre-optic cables and major Internet hubs, few Internet companies have adopted encryption for traffic exchange. It is rare that email is encrypted in transit or that data are stored in encrypted format with no access by the hosting provider. In any case, if content encryption is implemented, then because of the design of the Internet, it is difficult to obfuscate Internet traffic records with the intention to bypass blocking or monitoring except with the use of TOR networking (The Onion Router). TOR creates complex Internet traffic paths which then obfuscate the unique patterns of any single traffic pattern which are of interest. Unfettered access to primary international communication cables can support the possibility of decoding such obfuscated patterns.

Child Abuse Material

Let us review the challenges of detecting child abuse material with specific focus on images rather than text, voice or video. Such material must first be created, then distributed on the Internet, downloaded by interested parties and then stored and viewed. Each of these steps creates both online and offline digital fingerprints and records.

The camera, which records an illegal image, also records additional meta-data about the image which describes the technical photographic context when the image was recorded (light levels, indoor/outdoor, lens aperture and duration of exposure), and modern cameras can record GPS, camera model, camera serial number or camera configuration at the time the image was taken. Recent advances in camera sensors (which offer very high resolutions) permit the identification of a specific camera by calculating the almost unique "dna" of each camera where minor differences and variations on image processing capabilities can permit the identification of a camera by analysing publicly displayed photographs with non-public illegal images. The image of a modern digital camera is stored in a memory storage device which can also be forensically analysed for digital fingerprints. The image storage structure is different for different brands of cameras, and direct access to the storage media can yield many useful clues for a criminal investigation.

Once the image is created, the image will be distributed on the Internet. It might be first edited, changed or obfuscated using software or hardware to destroy, corrupt or delete digital fingerprints and, in extreme cases, this can be successful. However, even in these difficult cases, the computer where this work was conducted will contain forensic records of activities—software installed and used, image files accessed, files edited, use of Internet programmes and often detailed timeline of activities which occurred on the computer. Forensic analysis can detect image edits and updates (morphed images). The records of Internet access to upload the content onto the Internet creates a complex web of digital artefacts on the device used to upload the data from and also creates a complex range of log records on the local and intermediate Internet service providers.

The image can be accessed, viewed and downloaded from persons located across the world. There will be digital records and fingerprints on the intermediary service providers and the end-user Internet service provider and on the local network and the local device used to initiate the Internet activity.

The image can be stored in many different formats supplemented by compression, encryption or hiding techniques. It can be stored in many different types of media and with direct, indirect or no network access. It can be stored in cameras, tv recorders, game players, children's toys, health monitoring devices, etc. in addition to a wide variety of computing and mobile devices. Stored data do not have to be static and can be transferred across international and jurisdictional boundaries on random or regulated schedules or can be divided across many different international storage locations.

Of course, if it is possible to access computing devices remotely or if it is possible to have unrestricted access to network cables at a national and international level, then there are serious concerns about the level of trust which can be placed on digital evidence since with enough knowledge of computing systems and application structures available to digital forensic scientists, it would be possible to surreptitiously place believable difficult-to-refute evidence on any system and ensure the supporting traffic logs are recorded on intermediary systems.

If we study the actual images that are considered the image of a crime scene where the abuse of a child takes place, we need to work to determine several critical pieces of information from the image analysis. We need to identify the location where the image was taken. We need to identify the victim or victims in the photograph so that the victim can be rescued from a damaging situation and provided with treatment and support. We need to identify the perpetrators who committed the crime and the identity of the photographer if different. The image can be analysed to identify any known product brands in the image which can identify the continent, country and region or even shop where the product was sold and bought. For example, there was one image where the boxes of computers previously purchased were recorded in the image which almost offered a detailed view of a barcode of the purchaser account details. Another image when abuse occurred in a child's playground was identifiable from the type, range, colour and layout of the playground equipment. The image can contain artefacts of telephones, power sockets, newspapers, magazines, etc. which can be used to narrow down the search to a location for more traditional methods of investigation. The clothes worn by the victims and the shadows of the perpetrator can offer clues to the investigation.

These techniques described in the previous paragraphs apply to static text images, but there are evolving techniques that offer similar levels of forensic analysis for other types of content such as video, voice or text material.

Specifying Content

To specify which content is illegal or not illegal, there should be a trained and skilled expert making the evaluation of the alleged illegal content against a specific legislative provision. In the area of child pornography (the usual legal term for child abuse material), the major primary definitions are in the Council of Europe Conventions on Cybercrime and Protection of Children against Sexual Exploitation and Sexual Abuse and the European Commission Directive on Certain legal aspects of information society services, in particular electronic commerce and Directive 2011/93/EU of the European Parliament and of the Council on combating sexual abuse and sexual exploitation of children and child pornography. These documents are then supported by national law which defines the exact nature of child pornography and child abuse. Images, text, videos, voice and illegal activities are clearly defined, and any content on the Internet which is suspected of being child abuse material needs to be evaluated according to these standards. In an ideal world, content would be evaluated in a clearly specified judicial process, but due to the speed of movement on the Internet, such procedures, although still used for the prosecution of individuals, were found to be inadequate for content on the Internet. Often the material is initially assessed by the Internet hotlines created across the world which pass suspect material to law enforcement who make the determination whether material is likely to be illegal.

Today Interpol[34] and US NCMEC[35] (National Centre for Missing and Exploited Children) host a list of the worst images of child abuse which have been discovered and share this list of images with law enforcement agencies across the world. The national law enforcement agencies then share this list with trusted Internet service providers to enable them to detect the upload or download of such images from their networks.

When material is deemed to be illegal, attempts have been made to ensure that this material is not further re-distributed on the Internet using blocking technologies. The list of known illegal images is also used to make legal search and seizure and forensic analysis of computer networks, hosts and storage media faster by using the list to compare against currently hosted and stored files to determine if any known illegal images are among the seized or monitored material.

The creation of the list is an important role that requires oversight and accountability since it would be possible to include any type of material on the list and there have been accusations in the past that list maintained have included material on the list which is not illegal but might be considered to be inappropriate by conservatively minded individuals.

The list itself is a special technical challenge. In fact, there are several lists that exist for different Internet services.

There is a list of known keywords used by paedophiles to search for child abuse material on search engines. This list is distributed to search engine providers to prevent users from using their services to access illegal content.

There is a list of known websites which have regularly hosted illegal material. This list can be used both by search engine providers and by hosting providers and blacklisting inappropriate sites that are blocked by host-based anti-malware software. This list can include a list of IP addresses or domain names.

The third list is a list of known illegal images that have been detected during investigations by law enforcement across the world. It would not be legal or indeed morally appropriate to distribute the exact images of child abuse. Instead, alternative methods of specifying content are required. Such methods need to be precise and accurate so that they uniquely specify an image of known child abuse and cannot accidently refer to other legal content. The method is known as digital image fingerprinting. A fingerprint is a computer algorithm which calculates a one-way numerical code which uniquely identifies each specific image. The fingerprint unique code is compared against the calculated code for a suspect image. If the generated code matches one that is on the list of illegal content, then we can be sure that the images are identical.

One problem with the approach of seeking identical matches between images is that minor changes in the suspect image (cropping, resizing, re-colouring, etc.) means that the image fingerprints will be different from the ones on the list of

---

[34]http://www.interpol.int/Crime-areas/Crimes-against-children/Crimes-against-children (last accessed 4 Jan 2015).

[35]http://www.missingkids.com/Exploitation/Industry (last accessed 4 Jan 2015).

known illegal content. New approaches have been adopted to deal with such situations. One such technique is called PhotoDNA[36] developed by Microsoft Research in collaboration with Dartmouth College. According to Microsoft[37] *"PhotoDNA enables analysts to calculate the unique digital signature of an image and then match that signature against those of other photos. The PhotoDNA 'robust hashing' technique differs from other common hashing technologies because it does not require the image's characteristics to be completely identical to reliably find matches, thereby enabling matches to be identified even when photos are resized or similarly altered"*. Of course, when images are not directly matched using specific matching, any matches suggested by PhotoDNA software need to be verified by human eye for further criminal investigation.

Microsoft, Facebook and other international service providers now use PhotoDNA with lists provided by Interpol or NCMEC to compare all images uploaded to their services against the known list of illegal content. Any content that matches is forwarded to law enforcement for investigation.

As regards video content, there are separate techniques developed by Videntifier from Iceland[38] in collaboration with Interpol and others to create methods of uniquely identifying videos.

The major limitation of all these approaches is that they can only report on known content. They cannot easily detect new material that has not been seen before or investigated by law enforcement. However, there are initiatives to detect content which has not been seen before through complex image analysis with attempts to detect images based on skin tone, title and sharp analysis. Further details are available in the FIVES: Forensic Image and Video Examination Support[39] project description and iCop: Identifying and Catching Originators in P2P Networks.[40]

Whereas all these examples have used the area of child abuse as an example, many states are concerned about a diverse range of online content and activity. Many states are also concerned about extreme adult content, many are concerned about online incitement to terrorism, and many are concerned about illegal online drugs or gambling.

There are concerns that service providers are being drawn into areas of behaviour which are not sufficiently transparent or accountable and have a direct impact on human rights and rights to family life and rights to freedom of expression. In some countries, criticising the state is a criminal offence. The EDRI document

---

[36]http://www.microsoft.com/global/en-us/news/publishingimages/ImageGallery/Images/Infographics/PhotoDNA/flowchart_photodna_Web.jpg (last accessed 4 Jan 2015).

[37]http://www.microsoft.com/en-us/news/presskits/photodna/docs/PhotoDNAFS.doc (last accessed 4 Jan 2015).

[38]http://www.videntifier.com/news/article/advanced-video-and-image-analysis-in-interpol-child-abuse-database (last accessed 4 Jan 2015).

[39]http://ec.europa.eu/information_society/apps/projects/factsheet/index.cfm?project_ref=SIP-2008-TP-131801 (last accessed 4 Jan 2015).

[40]http://scc-sentinel.lancs.ac.uk/icop/ (last accessed 4 Jan 2015).

human rights and privatised law enforcement "looks at the extent to which 'voluntary' law enforcement measures by online companies are serving to undermine long-established fundamental rights principles and much of the democratic value of the Internet".[41]

Different Services

Not all Internet services are the same. It has been outlined earlier the complex range of services. Each service has different capabilities for oversight, monitoring and detecting criminal activity. Email is different from peer-to-peer, and social network websites are very different from search engine providers. Whereas many of these services play a role in combating illegal online activity and content, there are also many methods to evade detection and circumvent blocking initiatives.

Appendix I

List of Newsgroups from Metropolitan Police 26 August 1996 requested to be blocked.

```
alt.binaries.pictures.boys
alt.binaries.pictures.child.erotica.female
alt.binaries.pictures.child.erotica.male
alt.binaries.pictures.children
alt.binaries.pictures.erotic.children
alt.binaries.pictures.erotica child
alt.binaries.pictures.erotica.child.female
alt.binaries.pictures.erotica.child.male
alt.binaries.pictures.erotica.children
alt.binaries.pictures.erotica.lolita
alt.binaries.pictures.erotica.pre-teen
alt.binaries.pictures.erotica.teen.fuck
alt.binaries.pictures.erotica.young
alt.binaries.pictures.lolita.fucking
alt.binaries.pictures.lolita.misc
alt.sex.boys
alt.sex.children
alt.sex.fetish.tinygirls
alt.sex.girls
alt.sex.incest
```

---

[41]https://edri.org/human-rights-and-privatised-law-enforcement/ (last accessed 4 Jan 2015).

```
alt.sex.intergen
alt.sex.pedophile.mike-labbe
alt.sex.pedophilia.
alt.sex.pedophilia.boys
alt.sex.pedophilia.girls
alt.sex.pedophilia.swaps
alt.sex.pedophilia.pictures
alt.sex.pre-teens
alt.sex.teens
alt.sex.weight-gain
alt.fan.cock-sucking
alt.binaries.pictures.voyeurism
alt.binaries.pictures.lolita.fucking
alt.binaries.pictures.erotica.voyeurism
alt.binaries.pictures.erotica.young
alt.binaries.pictures.erotica.uniform
alt.binaries.pictures.erotica.urine
alt.binaries.pictures.erotica.teen.fuck
alt.binaries.pictures.erotica.uncut
alt.binaries.pictures.erotica.spanking
alt.binaries.pictures.erotica.teen.female.
masturbation
alt.binaries.pictures.erotica.pornstars
alt.binaries.pictures.erotica.pre-teen
alt.binaries.pictures.erotica.oral
alt.binaries.fetish.scat
alt.binaries.pictures.erotic.anime
alt.binaries.pictures.erotic.centerfolds
alt.binaries.pictures.erotic.senior-citizens
alt.binaries.pictures.erotica.animals
alt.binaries.pictures.erotica.art.pin-up
alt.binaries.pictures.erotica.breasts.small
alt.binaries.pictures.erotica.butts
alt.binaries.pictures.erotica.cheerleaders
alt.binaries.pictures.erotica.disney
alt.binaries.pictures.erotica.fetish.feet
alt.binaries.pictures.erotica.fetish.hair
alt.binaries.pictures.erotic.senior-citizens
alt.binaries.pictures.erotica.teen
alt.binaries.pictures.erotica.male.anal
alt.sex.pedophile.mike-labbe
alt.sex.masturbation
alt.sex.fetish.tickling
alt.sex.fetish.waifs
alt.sex.fetish.watersports
```

```
alt.sex.fetish.wrestling
alt.sex.first-time
alt.sex.fetish.girl.watchers
alt.sex.homosexual
alt.sex.incest
alt.sex.intergen
alt.sex.jp
alt.sex.magazines
alt.sex.masturbation
alt.sex.movies
alt.sex.necrophilia
alt.sex.pedophilia
alt.sex.pictures
alt.sex.pictures.female
alt.sex.pictures.male
alt.sex.services
alt.sex.spam
alt.sex.spanking
alt.sex.stories
alt.sex.strip-clubs
alt.magazines.pornographic
alt.magick.sex
alt.personals.spanking.punishment
alt.sex.
alt.sex.anal
alt.sex.bestiality
alt.sex.bondage
alt.sex.breast
alt.sex.enemas
alt.sex.exhibitionism
alt.sex.fat
alt.sex.fetish.diapers
alt.sex.fetish.fa
alt.sex.fetish.feet
alt.sex.fetish.hair
alt.sex.fetish.orientals
alt.binaries.multimedia.erotica
alt.binaries.pictures.boys
alt.binaries.pictures.children
alt.binaries.pictures.erotica
alt.binaries.pictures.erotica.amateur.d
alt.binaries.pictures.amateur.female
alt.binaries.pictures.amateur.male
alt.binaries.pictures.erotica.anime
alt.binaries.pictures.erotica.bestiality
```

```
alt.binaries.pictures.erotica.blondes
alt.binaries.pictures.erotica.bondage
alt.binaries.pictures.erotica.cartoons
alt.binaries.pictures.erotica.female
alt.binaries.pictures.erotica.furry
alt.binaries.pictures.erotica.gaymen
alt.binaries.pictures.erotica.male
alt.binaries.pictures.erotica.orientals
alt.binaries.pictures.erotica.pregnant
alt.binaries.pictures.erotica.teen
alt.binaries.pictures.erotica.teen.d
alt.binaries.pictures.girlfriend
alt.binaries.pictures.girlfriends
alt.binaries.pictures.girl
alt.binaries.pictures.horny.nurses
alt.binaries.pictures.pictures.nudism
alt.binaries.pictures.tasteless
alt.homosexual
alt.sex.swingers
alt.sex.telephone
alt.sex.trans
alt.sex.wanted
alt.sex.watersports
alt.sex.bestiality.pictures
alt.sex.children
alt.sex.cu-seeme
alt.sex.fetish.scat
alt.sex.fetish.tinygirls
alt.sex.fetish.wet-and-messy
alt.sex.oral
alt.sex.orgy
alt.sex.pedophilia.girls
alt.sex.pedophilia.pictures
alt.sex.pictures.d
alt.sex.stories.gay
alt.sex.stories.tg
alt.sex.super-size
alt.sex.tasteless
alt.sex.teens
alt.sex.video-swap
alt.binaries.pictures.erotica.black.male
alt.binaries.pictures.erotica.children
alt.sex.sm.fig
```

References

1. Akdeniz Y (1997) Governance of pornography and child pornography on the global internet: a multi-layered approach. In: Edwards L, Waelde C (eds) Law and the internet: regulating cyberspace. Hart Publishing, Oxford, pp 223–241
2. European Commission (1996) Illegal and harmful content on the internet. Communication from the Commission to the Council, the European Parliament, the Economic and Social Committee and the Committee of the Regions. COM (96) 487 final, 16 October 1996
3. Akdeniz Y (1997) 'Policing the Internet', Conference Report, 1997 (1) The Journal of Information, Law and Technology (JILT). http://elj.warwick.ac.uk/jilt/bookrev/97_1pol/. New citation as at 1/1/04: http://www2.warwick.ac.uk/fac/soc/law/elj/jilt/1997_1/akdeniz2/
4. Council of the European Union (1997) Resolution of the Council and of the Representatives of the Governments of the Member States, meeting within the Council of 17 February 1997 on illegal and harmful content on the Internet Official Journal C 070, 06/03/1997 P. 0001–0002
5. Clinton WJ, Gore Jr, A (1997) The global information infrastructure (GII)—The Framework. http://clinton4.nara.gov/WH/New/Commerce/read.html. Last accessed 8 Dec 2014
6. European Union Ministers (1997) European Ministerial Conference entitled "Global Information Networks: Realising the Potential", held in Bonn from 6–8 July 1997. Declaration available on http://web.mclink.it/MC8216/netmark/attach/bonn_en.htm#Heading01. Last accessed 7 Dec 2014
7. Department of Justice, Equality and Law Reform, Ireland (1998) Working Group on Illegal and Harmful Use of the Internet, First Report of the Working Group. http://www.justice.ie/en/JELR/Pages/Illegal_use_of_the_Internet_report. Last accessed Dec 14
8. European Parliament (2013), COM (2013) 48: Proposal for a Directive of the European Parliament and of the Council concerning measures to ensure a high common level of network and information security across the Union Available on http://eur-lex.europa.eu/procedure/EN/202368. Last accessed Dec 14
9. UNESCO (1999) Experts Meeting on Sexual Abuse of Children, Child Pornography and Paedophilia non the Internet : an international challenge UNESCO, Paris Room II, Background Document. (CII-98/CONF. 6051 (E) http://unesdoc.unesco.org/images/0011/001147/114751Eo.pdf. Last accessed 9 Dec 2014
10. European Parliament (1999) Decision No 276/1999/EC of the European Parliament and of the Council of 25 January 1999 adopting a multiannual Community action plan on promoting safer use of the Internet by combating illegal and harmful content on global networks. http://eur-lex.europa.eu/legal-content/EN/TXT/PDF/?uri=CELEX:31999D0276&from=EN. Last accessed 8 Dec 2014
11. European Parliament (2003) DECISION No 1151/2003/EC of the European Parliament and of the Council of 16 June 2003 amending Decision No 276/1999/EC adopting a multiannual Community action plan on promoting safer use of the Internet by combating illegal and harmful content on global networks http://eur-lex.europa.eu/legal-content/EN/TXT/PDF/?uri=CELEX:32003D1151&from=EN. Last accessed 8 Dec 2014
12. European Commission (2003) Communication from the Commission to the Council, the European Parliament, the European Economic and Social Committee and the Committee of the Regions concerning the evaluation of the Multiannual Community Action Plan on promoting safer use of the Internet and new online technologies by combating illegal and harmful content primarily in the area of the protection of children and minors 03.11.2003 COM(2003) 653 final. Available on http://eur-lex.europa.eu/legal-content/EN/TXT/PDF/?uri=CELEX:52003DC0653&from=EN. Last accessed 8 Dec 2014
13. European Parliament (2005) DECISION No 854/2005/EC of the European Parliament and of the Council of 11 May 2005 establishing a multiannual Community Programme on promoting safer use of the Internet and new online technologies available at http://eur-lex.europa.eu/legal-content/EN/TXT/PDF/?uri=CELEX:32005D0854&from=EN. Last accessed 8 Dec 2014

14. European Commission (2007) Communication from the Commission to the Council, the European Parliament, the European Economic and Social Committee and the Committee of the Regions COM/2007/0496 final—Available on http://eur-lex.europa.eu/legal-content/EN/TXT/?uri=CELEX:52007DC0496. Last accessed 14 Dec 2014

15. European Parliament (2000) Directive 2000/31/EC of the European Parliament and of the Council of 8 June 2000 on certain legal aspects of information society services, in particular electronic commerce. Official Journal L 178, 17/07/2000 P. 0001–0016. Available on http://eur-lex.europa.eu/LexUriServ/LexUriServ.do?uri=CELEX:32000L0031:en:HTML. Last accessed 14 Dec 2014

16. Council of Europe (2001) Convention on Cybercrime signed in Budapest on 23.XI.2001 (ETS No. 185) Available at http://conventions.coe.int/Treaty/EN/Treaties/Html/185.htm. Last accessed 14 Dec 2014

17. Bertelsmann Foundation (1999) Self-regulation of Internet Content by Dr, Marcel Machill and Jens Waltermann